Writing On The Line

20th Century W

GW00771754

An annotated list by
Sarah Richardson

Additional essays by
Merylyn Cherry, Sammy Palfrey
and Gail Chester

With an introduction by
Gilda O'Neill

Wo

Writing on the Line
20th Century Working-Class
Women Writers

Essays copyright © with individual authors
Book concept copyright © Sarah Richardson
Published 1996 by: Working Press,
54 Sharsted Street, SE17 3TN
Cover illustration and design: Matthew Richardson
Tel. 01874 636269
Printed by: Spiderweb Tel. 0171 281 3033
With thanks to: Stefan Szczelkun, Richard McKeever,
John Gorman and Richard Turner.
ISBN No. 1-870736-54-0

This book is dedicated to
working-class women
everywhere.

Contents

Introduction

By: Gilda O'Neill.

When I was invited to write this introduction to "Writing on the Line - Working-Class Women Writers of the 20th Century," I was both delighted and proud to say yes. Proud because I was being included in such illustrious company, and delighted because any writer would be honoured to introduce such a book.

That said, just because we appear in the same publication, I would hate the reader to fall into the trap of lumping all the writers together in a homogenous whole. The themes and concerns in our writing are as varied as we are. So, what then justifies linking us as writers?

I believe it is, in part at least, the fact that our work is informed by our specific class and gender experience. Nothing unusual in that, maybe. Isn't that what all writers do? Yes, but in the case of working-class women, our specific experiences can, if appropriately translated, give our writing a particular strength and power. This, in its many forms, can then validate, inform, give meaning to and explain our position in history, society and culture. In other words, it is this translation into the written word of our own understanding of the meaning of those experiences, which, if successful, gives a richness and variety specific to our class roots and gender. It can also make very entertaining reading!

Merylyn Cherry's essay "Towards Recognition of Working-Class Women Writers," both contextualises the booklist and explores in depth six of the writers. Sammy Palfrey's research "Writing in the Miner's Strike 1984-1985" documents the important role of women in the working-class literature produced by the strike. And Gail Chester's piece "Publishing - A Gentleperson's Profession?" offers a personal account of why working-class women have such difficulty in being published. I hope that the Annotated Booklist by Sarah Richardson encourages readers to look at some of their favourite writers with fresh eyes, and that it also prompts them to sample lots of new authors who, in their turn will become old favourites to be returned to, loved and cherished.

An Annotated List of Working-Class Women Writers

Sarah Richardson

Introduction.

This list of working-class women writers is intended to provoke discussion and debate, and not is not definitive. I have taken as my definition of class the author's class background and not subject matter or any other criterion such as political stance. Furthermore, all the authors listed here have produced at least one volume of fictional work (novel, poems or plays) or autobiography. Some women have also written essays or appeared in anthologies. All the women listed have been published at some time. The date that appears in brackets straight after the title is the original date of publication. If the book is still in print, an asterisk appears after this, and details of any prize won. In the case of poems and short stories, the title denotes a collection of work and not an individual piece. There is a selection of writers from groups within the Federation of Worker Writers and Community Publishers. It is intended to bring out a full list for the 20th Anniversary of the FWWCP. in 1996.

Linda Anderson 1949-

> To Stay Alive (1988*)
> Cuckoo (1988*)

■Born in Belfast and moved to England in 1972. "Cuckoo" is about a single mother with a mixed race child living in London.

Maya Angelou 1928-

Autobiography

> I Know Why the Caged Bird Sings (1969*)
> Gather Together in my Name (1974*)
> Singin' and Swingin' and Gettin' Merry Like Christmas (1976*)
> The Heart of a Woman (1985*)
> All God's Children Need Travelling Shoes (1987*)
> Wouldn't Take Nothin' For My Journey Now (1994*)

Poetry

> Now Sheba Sings a Song (1987*)
> And Still I Rise (1988*)
> Just Give Me a Cool Drink of Water Before I Die (1988*)
> I Shall Not Be Moved (1990*)

■Born in St. Louis, Missouri. After the break-up of parents she went to live with her younger brother at the home of her grandmother, a shopkeeper in Stamps, Arkansas. As a black child in the American South, she writes graphically and movingly of her experiences there, both of racism and the support of her family. As a girl of 8 she was raped, which left her mute for 5 years. Later she moved to California and gave birth to a son, aged 16. Subsequently she was a waitress, singer, actress, dancer, black activist and editor. She toured Africa with the cast of "Porgy and Bess" in the late 40's and then moved to New York to join the Harlem Writers Guild. She performed in Genet's "The Blacks." In the

1960's she became more closely involved with black struggles and spent several years in Ghana as editor of African Review.

Mary Antin 1881-1949

Letters
> From Plotz to Boston (1899)

Autobiography
> The Promised Land (1912)

Essays
> Those who knock on our gates: A Complete Gospel of Immigration. (1914)

■Born in Russia, emigrated in 1894 to Boston. Lived in slum-dwelling with family who worked in sweatshops. Had first poem published aged 15 and went on to become a teacher and pursue her interests in women's rights, liberal Judaism and transcendentalism.

Pat Arrowsmith 1930-

> Jericho (1965*)
> Somewhere Like This (1970*)
> The Prisoner (1982)

Poetry
> Breakout (1975)
> Thin Ice (1984)
> Nine Lives (1990*)

Autobiography
> I Should Have Been a Hornby Train (1992*)

Non-Fiction
> On the Brink (1981)

■Born in Warwickshire. Worked in a succession of unskilled jobs before moving onto social work and journalism. A campaigner, she worked and wrote for CND and civil liberties and against the British prescence in Northern Ireland and the Vietnam War. She has been jailed for political reasons.

Dorothy Bailey 1916-

Autobiography
>Children of the Green (1981*)

■Born and brought up in Bethnal Green, East London. Her book is a portrait of London between the wars.

Dorothy Baker 1907-1968

>Young Man with a Horn (1938)
>Trio (1943*)
>Our Gifted Son (1948)
>The Street (1951)
>Cassandra at the Wedding (1963*)

T.V. Drama
>The Ninth Day (1957).

■Born in Montgomery, USA. Father a railway worker. Lived in France as a young woman. Several unsuccessful attempts at writing until the publication of her first novel. Had two daughters and continued to write. Her second novel controversially explored alcoholism and sado-masochism. Her final one tells the story of twin girls, one conventionally married, the other a lesbian.

Toni Cade Bambara 1931-

>The Salt Eaters (1980*, American Book
>Award)

Short story collections
>Gorilla, My Love (1972*)
>The Sea Birds are Still Alive (1972*)

Editor and contributor
>The Black Woman (1970)
>Tales and Stories for Black Folks (1971)
>Southern Black Utterances Today (1975)

■Born in Harlem. As a child listened to street preachers and speakers which, together with the music of the period laid foundation for future work. Encouraged to write by mother. Has worked as a teacher, community worker, in the theatre, as a welfare investigator and writer-in-residence. "The Black Woman" was one of the earliest collections of feminist writing.

A.L. Barker 1918-
> Apology for a Hero (1950)
> A Case Examined (1965)
> A Heavy Feather(1978)

Short Stories
> Innocents:Variations on a Theme(1947)
> The Joy-Ride and After (1963)
> Femina Real (1971)
> Life Stories (1981)

■Born in Kent. Left school at sixteen to work as a secretary and later as a journalist. In the War, served in the Land Army and in the Fire Service. Has adapted some of her work for the screen.

Elizabeth Banks 1870-1938
Journalism
> All about Typewriter Girls (1891)
> Adventures of an American Girl in London (1894)
> The Almighty Dollar in London Society (1894)
> The Mystery of Frances Farrington (1909)
> The School for John and Mary (1925)
> The Re-making of an American (1928)

■Born in New Jersey. Orphaned at an early age she was brought up by an aunt and began working as a reporter in 1889 and published her first essay on working women in 1891. She then emigrated to Britain and continued to write about working life. She worked as a washerwoman, servant, flower-seller and crossing-sweeper (Adventures of American Girl). She investigated the selling of favours at court (The Almighty Dollar) which led to a tightening up of the system by Queen Victoria, still effective today.

She attacked the Judicial system in 1909 and the Class system in 1925. In her final essay she describes how, as a reporter, she turned an unsuspecting newspaper from anti-suffragette into one in favour of women's suffrage.

Pat Barker 1943-

Union Street (1982*, Fawcett Prize Winner)
Blow Your House Down (1984*)
Century's Daughter (1986*)
The Man Who Wasn't There (1989*)
Regeneration (1992*)
Eye in the Door (1993*)
The Ghost Road (1995*)

■Born at Thornaby-on-Tees and brought up by her grandmother. Went to the LSE. Had three unpublished novels until, while on a writing course, Angela Carter advised her to write historically and not of the present. The result was "Union Street" which won the Fawcett Prize. In this and subsequent books, the author says she taps into women's oral tradition. Her first novel is a series of 7 linked short stories about "Kelly" written in a vivid and realistic style. Her second novel is written about a group of prostitutes living in fear of a murderer. The third is about a woman relating her life and the last is about a young man growing up in an all female household and looking for male role models outside the family home.

Elizabeth Bartlett 1924-

Poetry

A Lifetime of Dying (1979)

■Born in Deal, Kent in a coal-mining area. She won a scholarship to grammar school, but left at 15 to work in a factory. Has also worked as a home-help, secretary and adult education tutor in hospitals and prisons. Her work combines personal, political and social themes, is realistic and proudly working-class.

Barbara Baynton 1857-1929

>Human Toll (1907)

Short Stories

>Bush Studies (1902*)

■Born in New South Wales, daughter of a carpenter. Her work focuses on the hardship of life in the Australian bush, particularly in the isolation of women. She wrote ahead of her time on issues of sexuality and religion.

Pat Beer 1924-

>Moon's Ottery (1978)

Poetry

>The Loss of the Magyar (1959)
>The Survivors (1963)
>Just like the Resurrection (1967)
>The Estuary (1971)
>Driving West (1975)
>Selected Poetry(1979)
>The Lie of the Land (1983)

Autobiography

>Mrs. Beer's House (1968)

Critical Studies

>Reader, I Married Him (1974)

■Born in Devon. Daughter of a railway clerk. Taught at home by her Mother, a Plymouth Brethren Member, and then at primary and grammar school and university. Lived in Italy in the 50's. Her poetry is often descriptive of the Devon countryside. As a child, because of her father's job she was entitled to free rail travel, so another recurring theme in her poetry is railway journeys.

Vera Bell. no DoB.

Short Stories

>14 Jamaican Short Stories (1950)

Poetry

>New Ships (1971, contributor)
>You'd Better Believe It (1973, contributor)

■Born in St. Ann's, Jamaica and educated at state girls school. Has worked for the Social Welfare Commission and as an editor. Studied in the US. She writes of Caribbean life, and the damage done to it in the past and present.

Louise Bennett 1919-
Poetry
>Dialect Verses (1942)
>Jamaican Humour in Dialect (1943)
>Selected Poems (1982).

Anancy stories,
>(1944, 1950, 1957, 1979.)

■Born in Kingston, Jamaica. Daughter of a dressmaker and a baker. Taught to write standard English poetry at state school, she began to write and perform in patois in the late 1930's. She appeared on Jamaican radio in 1943 and in "yard" theatre from 1938. She had a weekly column in "The Sunday Gleaner." Because she chose to write in patois, she found it difficult to find a publisher, despite her fame as a performer, and was barred from the Jamaican Poetry League from 1943-1960. She came to London in 1945 to study at RADA and in the 40's and 50's toured and performed in Britain and the US. She returned home in 1955 and worked for the Social Welfare Commission and continued to write, perform, collect folklore and broadcast. Her insistence on writing in patois at a time when it was deeply unfashionable and has been influential on younger black writers.

Mary Bethune 1875-1955
Journalism
>Aframerican Women's Journal (Editor, 1935)
>I'll Never Turn Back No More (1938)
>Certain Unalienable Rights (1944)
>My Last Will and Testament (1955)

■Born in South Carolina, the daughter of former slaves. Educated at a black mission school and Bible College. First ambition, to be an African Missionary, was unrealised. Founded mission schools in 1898 and 1904 which grew into the Bethune-Cookman College by 1928. She was its president from 1929 to 1942. She also headed the National Association of Coloured Women from 1924-1928 and advised President Roosevelt. Her writings call for racial equality and dignity.

Maeve Binchy 1940 -

Light a Penny Candle (1982*)
Echoes (1985)
Firefly Summer (1987)
Circle of Friends (1991*)

Collections of short stories

Victoria Line and Central Line (1978*)
Dublin 4 (1984*)
The Lilac Bus (1984*)
Silver Wedding (1988)

■Born in Dublin. Attended convent school and later graduated from University of Dublin. Writes on a wide range of Irish and British issues.

Sandra Birdsell 1942-

Chrome Street (1994*)

Linked short stories,

Night Travellers (1982)
Ladies of the House (1984)

■Born in Manitoba, US. Father a town barker. Mother had 19 pregnancies and 11 surviving children. Left school early, worked as a waitress. Writes from her experience as a mixed race child and also of inter-generational conflicts and women who missed out on Women's Liberation.

Marie Clare Blais 1939-

Mad Shadows (1959)
Tete Blanche (1960)
The Manuscripts of Pauline Archange (1970)
Les Apparences (1970)
Une Joualonais, sa Joualonie (1973)
Une Liason Parisienne (1975)

Short Stories

Le Sourd dans la ville (1979, Won Governor
General's award)
Visions d'Anna (1985)
Pierre, la Guerre du Printemps 81(1984)

■Born in Quebec City. Left convent school young to work in a shoe factory and then as an office worker. Went back to college later in life. Lived in USA, France and Quebec. Writes of lesbian and gay love, and also themes of drugs, the nuclear threat and ecological disaster.

Valerie Bloom 1956-

Poetry

Touch Me! Tell Me! (1983*)
Duppy Jamboree (1992*)

■Born in Clarendon, Jamaica into a family of storytellers. Like other Caribbean poets tried writing in standard English before finding her voice through patois. Worked as a librarian and teacher. Came to England in 1979. Is based in Manchester where performance is as important to her as writing. Uses the oral tradition to write for children, and write lyrics. Has been in several anthologies.

Capel Boake 1899-1944

Painted Clay (1917)
The Romany Mark (1922)
The Dark Thread (1936)
The Twig is Bent (1946)

Poetry

      Selected Poems (1949)

■Born in Sydney. Daughter of a photographer. Moved to Melbourne with family when she was 4. This was the city she wrote about in all her books, at a time when it was fashionable to write about the Bush and not urban life. Left school early to help support her family. She drew on her experience of shop and secretarial work in her first novel. Her second novel was a thriller and her third about a Jewish family.

Louise Bogan 1897-1970

Poetry

      Body of This Death (1923)
      Dark Summer (1929)
      Collected Poems (1941 and 1954)
      The Blue Estuaries (1969)

Letters

      What the Woman Lived (1973)

Autobiography

      Journey Around My Room (1980)

■Born in Maine to Irish parents. Went to Boston University to study but left to marry and have child. Found inspiration for her work from her sexual relationships. Had two breakdowns. Changed her attitude towards women and writing from anti-feminist in the 20's to pro-feminist in the 40's.

Julie Bovasso 1930-

Plays

      The Moon Dreamers (1967)
      Gloria and Esperanza (1968)
      Schubert's Last Serenade (1971)
      Down by the River where the Waterlilies are Disfigured Every Day (1972)
      The Nothing Kid (1975)
      Angelo's Wedding (1983)

Born in Brooklyn. Daughter of a truck driver. She first appeared on stage at the age of 13 and founded the Tempo Playhouse in 1953. It was a celebrated experimental theatre in the 50's. In 1972 she helped found the Women's Theatre Council to support women's plays.

Muriel Box 1905-

The Big Switch (1964)

Plays

Ladies Only (1934)

Petticoat Plays (1935)

Truth About Scotsmen (1938*)

Screenplays

The Seventh Veil (1946, Academy Award winner)

Biography

The Trial of Marie Stopes (1970)

Autobiography

Odd Woman Out (1974)

Born in New Malden. Educated at her local Board school, expelled from convent school and then went to Regent Street Polytechnic. Many of her early plays were written for all-women casts. Her plays and screenplays were often co-written with her husband, Sydney Box. In the '50's she directed films and in the '60's founded Femina Books.

Dionne Brand 1953-

Poetry

'Fore Day Morning (1978)

Earth Magic (1980)

Primitive Offensive (1982)

Winter Epigrams (1983)

Chronicles of the Hostile Sun (1984)

■Born in Trinidad. Studied at a girl's school and then at Toronto University. Much of her work draws on Caribbean and African history. She also gives readings on radio and TV.

Mona Brand 1915-

Plays

Here Under Heaven (1948)
Strangers in the Land (1955)
Our Dear Relations (1963)
Kisch (1983, for children).

■Born in Sydney, educated at Sydney Girls High. She worked in social welfare, research and teaching. She travelled and worked in Europe. Her work was often issue based, her first play dealing with racism and class struggle and later work being anti-colonial.

Rita Mae Browne 1944-

Rubyfruit Jungle (1973)
Six of the Best (1978)
Southern Discomfort (1982)
Sudden Death (1983)
High Hearts (1986)

Poetry

The Hand That Cradles the Rock (1971)
Songs to a Handsome Woman (1973),
Poems (1987)

■Born in Pennysylvania. Adopted by working-class parents who took her to Florida when she was 11. In 1965 she nearly starved, through poverty, but went on to get a degree from NY. University in 1968. Her first novel was initialy refused by publishers, but later welcomed by critics and the Women's Movement as a celebration of working-class lesbian life. She has continued to be radical and controversial in her work and active politically.

Mabel Burkholder 1881-1973

>The Course of Impatience Carningham
>(1911)
>Before the White Man Came (1923)
>Out of the Storied Past (1969)

■Born in Ontario. She taught and wrote articles for several publications. Her early work explored industrialisation and the exploitation of women in factories. She later wrote in favour of strike action and also recorded Canadian Indian legends.

Olivia Bush 1869-1944

Poetry

>Original Poems (1899)
>Driftwood (1914)

■Born on Long Island, New York. Of dual Indian-African heritage. Directed plays for a community centre in Boston, ran drama schools in Chicago and New York and wrote for magazines.

Mena Calthorpe 1905-

>The Dyehouse (1961)
>The Defectors (1969)
>Plain of Ala (1990*)

■Born in New South Wales. After a basic education she worked as a clerk, secretary and teacher. Her first novel is set in an urban factory and her second examines political power and corruption.

Maria Campbell 1940-

Autobiography

>Halfbreed (1973)

■Born in Saskatchewan. Left school at 12 to care for seven younger siblings on mother's death. Married at 15. Co-founded shelters for women. Autobiography charts struggle against poverty, racism, sexism, alcoholism and drug addiction.

Rosa Cappiello 1942-

I Semi Neri (1977)
Paese Fortunato (1977)

■Born in Naples, she emigrated to Australia in 1971. Wrote two novels with no formal education. Themes are living as migrant women in Australia, poverty, sexual and economic exploitation.

Ethel Carnie 1886-1962

Novels

Miss Nobody (1913)
Helen of the Four Gates (1917)
The House That Jill Built (1920)
The Marriage of Elizabeth (1920)
General Belinda (1923)
This Slavery (1925)
Eagle's Crag (1931)

Short Stories

The Lamp Girl and Other Stories (1913)
Voices of Womanhood (1915)

Poetry

Rhymes from the Factory (1907)
Songs of a Factory Girl (1911)

■Born in Lancashire. Daughter of cotton weavers. Worked herself in the cotton mill, half-time as a young child progressing to full-time at the age of 13. Worked for six months as editor of "Woman Worker" in 1909. After her marriage in 1915 she worked full time as a writer, in labour journalism and books.

Angela Carter 1940-1993.

Shadow Dance (1966)
The Magic Toyshop (1967* John Llewellyn Rhys memorial prize)
Several Perceptions (1968, Somerset Maugham award)

Heroes and Villains (1969*)
Love (1971*)
The Infernal Dream Machine of Dr.Hoffman
(1972*)
The Passion of the New Eve (1977*)
Nights at the Circus (1984*)
Wise Children (1992*)

Essays
Nothing Sacred (1982)

Short Stories
The Bloody Chamber (1979*)
Wayward Girls and Wicked Women (1986*)

History
The Sadeian Woman (1979*)
Black Venus (1986*)
Fireworks (1987*)
American Ghost (1993*)

■Born in London, she grew up in a South Yorkshire mining village. Went to grammar school in London, worked as a journalist and took a degree at Bristol where she cultivated her love of myth and legend, recurrent themes in her macabre work.

Alice Childress 1920-

A Hero Ain't Worth Nothin' But a Sandwich
(1973)
A Short Walk (1979*)
Rainbow Jordan (1983)
Those Other People (1989)

Plays
Trouble in Mind (1955)
Wedding Band (1966)
Wine in the Wilderness (1969)
String (1969)
Mojo, A Black Love Story (1970)
When the Rattlesnake Sounds (1975)
Let's hear it for the Queen (1976)

Sea Island Song (1979)
Gullah (1984).
Come Unto These Yellow Sands: 4 Plays
(1985*)

Satire

Like One of the Family (1956)

■Born in South Carolina and brought up in Harlem by her grandmother. A school drop-out, she taught herself to write. She wrote about issues which were controversial in their time, such as inter-racial marriage and had some difficulty getting her plays produced because of this. She also used black history in her work, such as Marcus Garvey.

Lucille Clifton 1936-

Poetry

Good Times (1969)
Good News About the Earth (1972)
An Ordinary Woman (1974)
Two-Headed Woman (1980)
Next (1987)
Good Woman (1987)

■Born in New York. Won a scholarship to Howard University, but dropped out after two years. Did teacher training. Had first book of poetry published, to critical acclaim when she had six children under 10. Writes from an inner-city and black perspective.

Catherine Cookson 1906-

Kate Hannigan (1950*)
The Mary Ann series (Seven titles, 1954-67*)
The Mallens (Four titles, 1973-4*)
The Round Tower (1968*, Winifred Holtby
Prize) and many others.

Autobiographies

Our Kate (1969*)
Catherine Cookson Country (1986*)

Poetry
> Let Me Make Myself Plain (1988*)

■Born in South Shields the illegitimate daughter of a servant and an un-named "gentleman". For most of her childhood she believed her mother was her sister. Brought up Catholic, she went to school until she was 14 and then went into service. She later worked in a laundry. Despite poor physical and mental health (she was unable to have children and has had several breakdowns) she is a very prolific writer. Her work is popular, sometimes historical and often based around a strong female, working-class character who overcomes obstacles and triumphs in the end.

Sarah Daniels 1957-
Plays
> Penumbra (1981)
> Ma's Flesh is Grass (1981)
> Ripen Our Darkness (1981)
> The Devil's Gateway (1983)
> Masterpieces (1983)
> Neaptide (1986)
> Byrthrite (1986)
> Gut Girls (1988*)
> Beside Herself (1991*)

■Born in London, she worked as a clerical assistant before writing plays. She explores topical issues in her work, such as Greenham Common, pornography and male violence as well as looking at working women's role historically in her most recent play.

Shelagh Delaney 1939-
Plays
> A Taste of Honey (1958* New York Drama Critics Award)
> The Lion in Love (1960)

Screenplays
> A Taste of Honey (1961*)
> The White Bus (1966)
> Charley Bubbles (1968)
> Dance With a Stranger (1985)

Plays for TV
> St. Martin's Summer (1974)
> Find Me First (1979)
> The House That Jack Built (1977)

Autobiographical short stories
> Sweetly Sings The Donkey (1963)

■Born in Salford, Lancashire. Daughter of a bus-inspector, she failed the 11-plus and went to secondary modern school, before transferring later to grammar and passing exams at the age of 16. She left school at 16 and worked as a shop-assistant, usherette and photographic assistant in order to support herself in writing. Her first play was produced at Stratford East in 1968. It told the story of a young, single mother and her relationship with a young man who is coming out. The social-realism of the piece linked her name with John Osborne and Arnold Wesker, and was seen as a reaction to the contrived drama of the pre-war years. Her other well-known drama is the screenplay to the acclaimed film "Dance With a Stranger", the carefully researched story of Ruth Ellis, the last woman in England to be hanged for murder.

Jean Devanny 1864-1962
> The Butcher Shop (1926)
> Leonore Divine (1926)
> Dawn Beloved (1928)
> Riven (1929)
> All For Love (1932)
> Paradise Flow (1935)
> The Ghost Wife (1935)
> Sugar Heaven (1936)
> Roll Back The Night (1945)

Non-fiction

By Tropic Sea and Jungle (1944)

Bird of Paradise (1945)

Cindie (1949)

Travels in North Queensland (1951)

Short stories

Old Savage (1927)

Autobiography

Point of Departure (1986)

Play

Paradise Flow (1985)

■Born in New Zealand. Daughter of a boiler-maker, she had little formal schooling, but educated herself by reading widely. Her first novel was banned for its being too explicit in its use of violence and discussion of sexuality. She moved to Australia in 1929 and joined the Communist Party. She was expelled 1940-1944 for her feminist beliefs. She helped found The Writers League. Her work deals with the big issues of women in the family and the struggle against class and sexual oppression. She also wrote considerably (both in fiction and non-fiction) about the canefields and the strikes of the 1930's.

Diane Di Prima 1934-

Poetry

More than 25 books, including:

Pieces of a Song (1990*)

■Born in Brooklyn. Went to Swathmore College and then became one of the few women "Beat" poets (with Jack Kerouac, Allen Ginsberg etc.) She has written twenty-five books of poetry and plays.

Patricia Dobler No DoB.

Poetry

anthologised in Working Classics (1990*)

Talking to Strangers (1986)

■Born in Ohio. Father was a steelworker, which her poems reflect. Now lives in Pittsburgh.

Carol Ann Duffy 1955-

Poetry

Flesh Weathercock (1973)
Fifth Last Song (1983*)
Standing Female Nude (1985)
Selling Manhattan (1987*)
Thrown Voices (1988)
Other Country (1990*)
Manchester Poetry (1990*)
Mean Time (1993)

Plays

Take My Husband (1982)
Cavern of Dreams (1984)
Loss (1986)
Little Women, Big Boys (1986)
William and the Ex-Prime Minister (1992*)

■Born in Glasgow and brought up in Staffordshire. Her work is often of the outsider in society. She has worked extensively in schools.

Maureen Duffy 1933-

That's How it Was (1962)
The Single Eye (1964)
The Microcosm (1966*)
The Paradox Players (1967)
Love Child (1971*)
I Want to Go to Moscow (1973*)
Capital (1975)
Gor Saga (1981)
Change (1987*)
Illuminations (1991*)

Plays

Rites (1969)
Solo (1970)

Old Time (1970)
A Nightingale in Bloomsbury Square (1974)
Londoners (1983*)
Wounds (1984*)
Housespy (1979*)
Occam's Razor (1993*)

Poetry
Collected Poems 1949-1984 (1985)
Non-fiction
The Passionate Shepherdess (1977)
The Erotic World of Faery (1977)

■Born in Wiltshire. Educated at state school and Kings College London. Her first novel is semi-autobiographical, about the intense relationship between a working-class woman and her illegitimate daughter. Her fictional work often explores themes of class, sexuality and gender in a realistic and fantastic way. She was the co-founder of The Writers Action Group in 1972. In her non-fiction she revived interest in the playwright Aphra Behn.

Jane Duncan 1910-1976
My Friend (1959-76* Nineteen books)
Jean Robertson (1969-75 Four books)
Books for children
Cameron (1963-8 Five books)

■Born in Dunbartonshire. Daughter of a policeman. Educated at Glasgow University, she worked as a secretary and during World War 2 in the WAAF. She lived in the West Indies from 1948-1958. Her books draw largely on her Scottish upbringing.

Grazia Deledda 1871-?
Cosima (Reprinted 1991*)
Elias Portalu (Reprinted 1991*)
After the Divorce (Reprinted 1985*)
Woman and the Priest (Reprinted 1987*)
Edera (Reprinted 1991*)

28

■Born in Sardinia. Wrote about rural Sardinia at a time when many Sardinians were basic subsistence farmers or agricultural labourers. Won the Nobel prize for Literature in 1926.

Nicky Edwards 1958-

Mud (1986*)
Stealing Time (1990*)
Tough at the Top (1993*)

Non-Fiction

Greenham Common: Women at the Wire (1984, contributor)

■A lesbian feminist and peace campaigner. Her first book explores reactions to war and peace through its various characters.

Buchi Emecheta 1944-

The Bride Price (1976*)
In the Ditch (1972)
Second Class Citizen (1974*)
The Slave Girl (1977*)
The Joys of Motherhood (1979*)
Destination Biafra (1981)
Double Yoke (1982*)
The Rape of Shavi (1983*)
Head Above Water (1986*)

■Born in Lagos, Nigeria. Daughter of a railway porter. Orphaned at an early age. Won a scholarship at ten to a Methodist school where she had to pray to ask forgiveness for wanting to be a writer. At seventeen left school, married and had a child. Came to Britain. At twenty-two left her husband (who burnt the manuscript of her first novel) and began studying for a degree, whilst supporting five children. Continued writing in the early morning before the children awoke. Her first three novels in particular focus on the personal struggle of those years, living on the dole. Later, her work broadened to explore the role of Nigerian women.

Barbara Ferland 1919-
Poetry
> The Penguin Book of Caribbean Verse
> (1986*, as a contributor)

■Born in Jamaica. Moved to Britain to work for the British Council and contribute to the radio programme "Caribbean Voices."

Leila Florence 1887-1966
Non-fiction
> We did not Fight (1935,as a contributor)
> My Goodness! My Passport (1942)
> Only an Ocean Between (1943)
> Our Private Lives (1944)
> Diary in letters 1915-1922 (1978)

■Born in Michigan. Father deserted family when young. Left school and became journalist, working on the Peace Ship in 1915. Moved to England in 1917.

Elizabeth Gurley Flynn 1890-1964
Non-fiction
> Women in the War (1942)
> Women have a Date with Destiny (1944)
> Women's Place (1947)
> I Speak my Piece (1955)
> The Anderson Story (1963)

■Born in New Hampshire. Daughter of a stone-cutter. Both parents socialists, mother advocated votes for women. Went to school in the Bronx, but dropped out to work for a socialist group. Worked for her socialist and feminist ideals all her life. Her two marriages broke up over her refusal to curb her political activity. She joined the Communist Party in 1936 and became its first woman chair in 1961. She died in Moscow.

Carolyn Forche No DoB.

Poetry

>Gathering The Tribes (1976*)
>The Country Between Us (1982*)

■Born in Detroit and brought up in Michigan. Daughter of a die-maker. Politically active, she campaigned for Vietnam, El Salvador and South Africa.

Margaret Forster 1938-

>Dames Delight (1964)
>Georgy Girl (1965*, made into a film)
>The Travels of Maudie Tipstaff (1967)
>Mr. Bone's Retreat (1971)
>The Seduction of Mrs. Pendlebury (1974*)
>Mother, Can You Hear Me? (1979*)
>Marital Rites (1981)
>Private Papers (1986*)
>Have The Men Had Enough? (1989*)
>Lady's Maid (1990*)
>The Battle for Christabel (1992*)

Non-fiction

>Significant Sisters(1984*)

Biographies

>The Rash Adventurer-Prince Charles Stuart (1973)
>Thackeray (1978)
>Elizabeth Barrett Browning (1988*)
>Daphne du Maurier (1993*)

■Born in Carlisle. Daughter of a fitter, she went to Carlisle Girls' School and won a scholarship to Oxford. She worked as a teacher and later as a reviewer and on boards for the BBC and Arts Council. Her novels examine, with wry humour, different aspects of familial relationships.

Janet Frame 1924-

Owls Do Cry (1957*)
Faces in the Water (1961*)
The Edge of the Alphabet (1962)
Scented Gardens for the Blind (1963)
The Adaptable Man (1965)
A State of Siege (1967)
The Rainbirds (1968)
Intensive Care (1970)
Living in the Manioto (1979*)
Scented Gardens for the Blind (1982)
The Carpathians (1988)
State of Siege (1990*)
Moon Minim (1993*)

Short stories

The Lagoon (1951*)
You are now Entering the Human Heart
(1984*)

Poetry

The Pocket Mirror (1967*)

Autobiography

To The Island (1982)
An Angel at my Table (1984)
The Envoy from Mirror City (1985)

■Born in Dunedin, New Zealand. Daughter of a railwayman and a mother who wrote for pleasure. She had a full and happy rural childhood with four siblings. Her fertile imagination was nurtured by childhood games. In her 'teens she was greatly saddened by the death by drowning of two of her sisters in separate incidents. She won a scholarship to college where, in an incredible act of classism, a lecturer mistook her shyness due to bad teeth and new surroundings as mental illness and had her committed to a mental institution. For eight years she was incarcerated and was subjected to numerous doses of electro-convulsive treatment. She wrote during this time, and towards the end of her stay her first book was published. The critical acclaim of it helped convince the authorities that she was sane and gain her release. After travelling in England and Spain, and gaining personal and writing experience, she returned to New Zealand to live near her family and continue to write. Her early books explore her experiences in mental institutions and her later ones are more in the realm of the imagination. Her three books of autobiography were made into a film by Jane Campion, "An Angel at my Table".

Gilly Fraser 1940-

Plays
> Do a Dance for Daddy (1976)
> A Bit of Rough (1977)
> I Can Give You a Good Time (1981)

Radio plays
> Playmates (1980)
> Bracelet (1980)
> Somewhere Else (1983)
> A Quick Visit Home (1984)

Plays for children
> Blame it on the Boogie (1980)
> Domestic Affair (1981)

TV. Play
> Not for the Likes of Us (1980)

■Born in Leeds. Left school at 16 to work with Northern Theatre school. Won a scholarship to Guildhall and began acting full time. Writes from own experience. She also wrote episodes for "Angels" and "Eastenders" on TV.

Tess Gallagher No DoB.

Poetry
> Under Stars (1987)
> Amplitude (1988)
> Moon Crossing Bridge (1992)
> My Black Horse (1995)

Portable Kisses (1995)

Anthologised in "Working Classics" (1990*)

■Born and brought up in a logging camp near Washington. Father was logger. She now teaches at Syracuse University.

Mary Gawthorpe 1881-1960

Pamphlets

Votes for Women (1910)

Editor

Labour News (No date)

The Freewoman (No date)

Autobiography

Up Hill to Holloway (1962)

■Born in Leeds. Daughter of mill worker/dressmaker and leather worker. From 13 worked as a pupil-teacher and later turned down the opportunity to go to teacher training college in order to support the family, her father having left. Involved in the Labour movement and with women's suffrage. Imprisoned for her beliefs in 1906.

Pam Gems 1925-

Plays

A Builder by Trade (1961)

My Warren(1973)

After Birthday (1973)

Dusa, Fish, Stas and Vi (1978*)

The Treat (1982)

Aunt Mary (1982)

Loving Women (1984)

Mrs. Frampton (1991*)

■Born in the New Forest. Father died in a workhouse when she was four. Was in the WRNS. during World War 2. Settled in the Isle of Wight. Had four children, one of whom has Down's Syndrome which she said helped bring her into the Women's Movement. She writes of eveyday life with black humour.

Barbara Giles 1912-

Poetry

Eve Rejects Apple (1978)

Earth and Solitude (1983)

Books for children

My Animal Friends (1981)

People and Places (1981)

Bicycles Don't Fly (1982)

■Born in Manchester and educated in Liverpool. Emigrated to Australia with her parents in 1923. Unable to complete her education due to poverty, she worked as a teacher and completed a degree in 1968 at the age of 56. Her poems are strongly feminist.

Ruth Gordon 1896-1985

Shady Lady (1983)

Plays

Over 21 (1940, filmed 1945)

Years Ago (1947)

A Very Rich Woman (1965)

Screenplays

A Double Life (1948)

Pat and Mike (1950)

The Marrying Kind (1951)

Adam's Rib (1952)

All written with husband Garson Kanin.

Autobiography

Myself Among Others (1971)

My Side (1976)

An Open Book (1980)

■Born in Massachusetts, daughter of a factory foreman. Had a long and successful stage career, while at the same time writing and collaborating. Her autobiographies read as excitingly as a film script.

Rosa Guy 1925-

Bird at my Window (1966*)
A Measure of Time (1983*)
My Love, My Love (1987*)
New Guys Around the Block (1983*)

Plays

Venetian Blinds (1954)

■Born in Trinidad, moved to New York in 1932, aged seven. At sixteen married, had son and worked in a clothing factory. Wrote and acted in black plays. Co-founded the Harlem Writers Guild. With Maya Angelou and Paule Marshall staged a sit-in by the Guild of the UN. when President Lumumba was assasinated in 1961. She returned to live in Trinidad for some years in the 1970's and has travelled widely. She writes of black experience in the US. and the Caribbean and of the civil rights movement.

Joy Harjo 1951-

Poetry

The Last Song (1975)
What Moon Drove me to This? (1980)
She Had Some Horses (1983*)
Secrets from the Centre (1989*)

■Born in Oklahoma to Native American parents. She has been active in the cause of Native Americans, for example on the National Association of Third World Writers. She is currently working on an anthology of Native women writers from North, Central and South America.

Bertha Harris 1937-

Catching Saradove (1969)
Confessions of Cherubino (1972)
Lover (1976)

Non-Fiction
>The Joy of Lesbian Sex (1977)
>(written with Emily Sisley)

■Born in North Carolina. Daughter of a salesman. Went to University, then moved to New York, where she did clerical jobs for five years. Her work reflects her Southern background and her discovery of Greenwich Village lifestyle. "Lesbian Sex" was the first commercially produced book on the subject. She has done teaching, editing and proof-reading.

Diana Hartog 1942-

Poetry
>Matinee Light (1983)
>Candy From Strangers (1986).

■Born in California and brought up in the Sierra Nevada mountains. Went to San Francisco State University. Moved to British Columbia in 1971 where she built a wooden house for herself and her daughter. Writes lyric poetry.

Gwen Hauser 1944-

Poetry
>Poems from the Sun-Dance (1972)
>Hands Get Lonely Sometimes (1974)
>The Ordinary Invisible Woman (1978)
>Danger, Women at Work (1979)
>Anthologised in Working Classics (1990*)

■Born in Alberta. Has done various sorts of factory work, waitressing, sorting post and Life modelling. Poetry is angry and extremely political.

Evelyn Haythorne No DoB.

Autobiography/History
>In Our Backs" (1986*)
>On Earth To Make the Numbers Up (1991*)

■Born and brought up in a pit village in the '30's. Her story has been re-told in three plays, as a TV. Profile and as an Open University study document as well as in written form.

Bessie Head 1937-1986

>When Rain Clouds Gather (1969*)
>Maru (1971*)
>A Question of Power (1973*)
>Serowe: Village of the Rain-Wind (1981*)
>A Bewitched Crossroad (1984)

Autobiography
>Women Alone (1990*)

Short stories
>Tales of Tenderness and Power (1990*)
>Collector of Treasures (1993*)

■Born in South Africa. Mother was wealthy and white but confined to a mental hospital until her death for becoming pregnant by a Zulu stable hand. She was taken from her mother at birth and brought up by foster parents. She did teacher training and became politically active in Nationalist politics, writing for "Drum" magazine. In 1971 she had a serious breakdown. Her work was ground-breaking. She was working on an autobiography when she died.

Dorothy Hewett 1923-

>Bobbin' Up (1959)

Plays
>This Old Man Comes Rolling Home (1976)
>Bon-bons and roses for Dolly (1976)
>The Golden Oldies (1976)
>The Tatty Hollow Story (1976)
>The Man from Mukinupin (1979)

■Born in Perth, Australia. Brought up on a wheat farm, and educated till the age of 12 by correspondence courses. Began to write at an early age. Joined the

Communist Party aged 19. Suicide attempt at 21. Married and had son who died and marriage broke up. Moved to Perth in 1949 and worked in factories. Used these experiences in her novel and first play. Very active in Communist party in 50's. Completed a degree in 1961 at the age of 38. Her later plays became more strongly feminist and fantastic.

Lilian Hellman 1905-1984
Screenplays
>The Children's Hour (1934)
>Days to Come (1936)
>Little Foxes (1939)
>Watch on the Rhine (1941)
>The Searching Wind (1944)
>Another Part of the Forest (1947)
>The Autumn Garden (1951)
>Toys in the Attic (1960)

Autobiograpy
>An Unfinished Woman (1969)
>Pentimento (1973, made into film "Julia")
>Scoundrel Time (1976)

She has also adapted work and edited letters.

■Born in New Orleans and brought up in New York. Daughter of a salesman. Lived with detective novelist Dashiell Hammett for many years until his death in 1961. Used themes which were unusual in their time, such as lesbianism and labour struggles.

Helen Hodgman 1945-
>Blue Skies (1976*)
>Jack and Jill (1978*)
>Broken Words (1989)

■Born in Aberdeen. Daughter of a gas-fitter. Emigrated to Tasmania with family in 1958 at the age of 13. Left school at 15 to work in a bank. In the 1970's came back

to Britain and worked as a cleaner and as a bookie until
her first novel was published.

Debbie Horsfield 1955-

Plays

>Out on the Floor (1981)
>Away from it All (1982)
>All You Deserve (1983)
>Touch and Go (1984)
>Revelations (1985)
>The Red Devils Trilogy (1986)

Radio Play

>Arrangements (1981)

TV. Series

>Making Out (1989)

■Born in Manchester. Went to Newcastle University.
Plays are often about young women, from the first about
teenage pregnancy and a shot-gun wedding to her most
successful trilogy, following the lives of four young,
Mancunian women.

Corinne Jacker 1933-

Plays

>Bits and Pieces (1973)
>Breakfast, Lunch, Dinner (1975)
>Harry Outside (1975)
>Travellers (1976, a musical)
>My Life (1977)
>Later (1979)

■Born in Chicago. Daughter of a Jewish plumber. A
precocious child, she wrote a play at nine and adapted
Chekhov at eleven. However, as an adult she experienced
a lot of sexism and classism in trying to be a director in
the late 50's and so gave it up to write science books in
the 60's. She only began writing when she believed she
had cancer. She has won several awards.

Naomi Jacob 1864-1964

>Jacob Usher (1925)
>The House of Gollantz (1930-1939)
>(seven books)

and over seventy more novels.

■Born in Yorkshire. Went to a church school, but left to work for an actress due to lack of money. Became an actress and a suffragette. Worked in a munitions factory during World War 1. Contracted TB. which halted her stage career and began to write under the pseudonym Ellington Gray. Moved to Italy in 1930 due to ill-health.

Meiling Jin 1956-

Poetry

>Gifts from my Grandmother (1985*)

■Born in Guyana to Chinese parents, the family came to Britain in 1964 to escape the politically unstable situation. The family lived seven to a room, which the author found comforting after her experiences of racism at school. Read to escape, first the classics and later modern black women writers which helped her find her own voice.

Gayl Jones 1949-

>Corregidora (1975*)
>Eva's Man (1976)

Plays

>Chile Woman (1974)

Poetry

>Song for Anninho (1981)
>The Hermit Woman (1983)
>Xarque (1985)

Short stories

>White Rat (1977)

■Born in Kentucky. Daughter of a cook. Her mother and grandmother were story-tellers. She was educated at a segregated school, later took a degree at Connecticut University. Her work deals with race, class and gender and is often set in the Southern States, though sometimes fantastic.

June Jordan 1936-

His Own Where (1971)

Poetry

Who Look at Me (1969)
Some Changes (1971)
New Days (1973)
Things I Do in the Dark (1977)
Passion (1980)
Lyrical Campaigns (1989)
Haruko and Other Love Poems (1993)

Essays

Moving Towards Home (1989*)
Technical Difficulties (1993*)

Biography

Fannie Lou Hamer (1972)

■Born in Harlem. Daughter of a nurse and a postman. Started writing at seven. Went to college in the early 50's, but dropped out when there were no black authors or women authors taught on the course. Worked as a journalist, designer, black film producer and involved actively in political campaigns.

Patricia Joudry 1921-

The Dweller on the Threshold (1973)
Spirit River to Angel's Roost (1977)
A Very Modest Orgy (1981)

Plays

Teach Me How to Cry (1955)
The Sand Castle (1955)
Three Rings For Michelle (1956)
Walk Alone Together (1960)

Semi-Detached (1960)

And The Children Played (1975)

Radio Plays

Going Up Please (1939)

Penny's Diary (1940)

The Aldrich Family (1945, co-authored)

Affectionately, Jenny (1951)

■Born in Alberta and brought up in Montreal. Wrote and acted at school. At 18 got first job working a lift, which she used as the basis of her first radio play. Moved to Britain in 1962, when she began to write in forms other than drama.

Jackie Kay 1961-

Poetry

The Adoption Papers (1991*)

Plays

Chiaroscuro (1986)

Twice Over (1988)

Other Lovers (1993*)

■Born in Edinburgh and brought up in Glasgow. Her book of poems chart her life, as a black child adopted by white parents, through to the present and issues of sexuality, Scottishness and being working-class.

Edith Kelley 1884-1956

Weeds (1923*)

The Devil's Hand (posthumously, 1974)

■Born in Toronto where she went to University. After graduating, worked on a commune. Supported self, husband and two young children by writing magazine stories. Later, worked on a tobacco farm, the experience of which she fictionalised in her first novel. Although well reviewed, it did not make money and she continued to do manual work such as cleaning throughout her life.

Annie Kenney 1879-1953

Memories of a Militant (1924)

■Born in Lancashire. Daughter of a mill-worker, one of 12 children. Worked half-time at the mill from the age of 10, and full-time from 13. In 1905 she joined the suffrage movement, wrote pamphlets and was imprisoned for her beliefs. Later, she did a correspondence course from Ruskin College and lectured during World War 1 in Australia and the US.

Jessie Kesson 1916-1994

The White Bird Passes (1959* filmed)
The Glitter of Mica (1963*)
Another Time, Another Place (1983* filmed)
Where the Apple Ripens (1985*)

■Born in a workhouse in Inverness. Brought up by single mother until the age of nine when she was sent to an orphanage because her mother was too ill to look after her. Developed an interest in writing at school. Left at 16 to become a housemaid but was later sacked. She had a breakdown and spent some time in mental hospital. She met and married a farm-labourer in 1936 and from then until she moved to London in 1954 was seen as an eccentric, by being a working-class writer. After their move to London she worked in Woolworths to support herself, and worked with children and the elderly. Her work reflects the struggles in her life - to conform and not be taken seriously, or to rebel and be ostracised.

Jamaica Kincaid 1949-

Small Place (1988*)
Lucy (1991*)
Autobiographical novel
Annie John (1985)
Poetry
At the Bottom of a River (1983)

■Born in Antigua of dual Indian/African heritage. Her mother encouraged her to write. Worked as a seamstress, and migrated to the US. in 1966. Attended college in New Hampshire. Her work has appeared in several magazines.

Irene Klepfisz 1941-
Poetry
> Periods of Stress (1975)
> Keeper of Accounts (1982)

■Born in Warsaw. Father died in the Warsaw Ghetto uprising when she was two. Smuggled out of Poland by peasants, she arrived in New York in 1949 with her mother and was educated there. She studied at the University of Chicago and did clerical work. Her work explores being lesbian, Jewish and the Holocaust.

Myrna Lamb 1930-
Collected Plays
> The Mod Donna and Scylon Z (1971)

■Born in New Jersey. Daughter of a member of the National Guard. Married and had a child at 19. Worked as an actress. Became involved in the civil rights' movement in the 60's and did further study. Her plays are feminist, and were often first produced for campaigning groups.

Rose Lane 1887-1968
> Hillbilly (1925)
> Let the Hurricane Roar (1933*)
> Free Land (1938)

Short stories
> Old Home Town (1935*)

Autobiography
> Her Story (1977*)

■Born in South Dakota. Daughter of Laura Ingalls

Wilder (cf.). Educated in a one-room school and left to become a telegraph operator. Later became a reporter and travel-writer. Her fictional work was set in the Mid-West.

Kate Llewelyn 1940-
Poetry
> Trader Kate and the Elephants (1982)
> Luxury (1985)
> Honey (1988)
> Dear You (1988)

Journal
> The Waterlily (1987)

■Born in South Australia. Worked as a nurse before gaining recognition for her poetry.

Audre Lorde 1934- 1993
Poetry
> First Cities (1968)
> Cables to Rage (1970)
> New York Head Shop (1975)
> Coal (1976)
> The Black Unicorn (1978*)
> Chosen Poems(1982*)
> Our Dead Behind Us (1986*)
> Undersong (1993*)

Autobiography
> The Cancer Diaries (1992*)
> Zami (1982*)

Essays
> Sister Outsider (1984*)
> A Burst of Light (1988*)

■Born in Harlem. Parents from Grenada. Went to college, worked as a librarian. Her work focuses on being black and a lesbian and the struggles this involves.

Pat Lowther 1935-1975
Poetry
> This Difficult Flowering (1968)
> The Age of the Bird (1972)
> Milk Stone (1974)
> A Stone Diary (1977*)

■Born in Vancouver. Daughter of a caretaker. Left school at 16 to work as a keypunch operator, but wrote and was actively involved in politics at the same time. Lived in poverty, had several children, her second husband was convicted of murder and died in prison. Her early work deals with motherhood and socialism, her later work with the environment.

Carrie Lumsden 1912-
Autobiography
> My Popular Eastenders (1991*)

■Born and brought up in the East End of London. Lived above a Rag and Bone shop. Father was in the 1st World War, she didn't meet him until 1919.

Shena McKay 1945-
> Dust Falls on Eugene Schlumberger (1964)
> Toddler on the Run (1964)
> Music Upstairs (1965),
> Old Crow (1967)
> An Advent Calendar (1971)
> Redhill Rococco (1986)

Short stories
> Babies in Rhinestones (1983)
> Dreams of Dead Women's Handbags (1987)

■Born in Edinburgh. Educated at a comprehensive and a grammar school. Left school at 16 to work in a library and then a factory and a shop. Wrote first novel aged 17. Her work is sometimes macabre and surreal, later work is gentler.

Margaret Mahy 1936-

Children's Fiction

> The Haunting (1983* won the Carnegie
> Award) and over forty others.

■Born in New Zealand. Daughter of a bridge-builder.
Did a degree and worked in a library. Her early work was
rejected by New Zealand publishers until an American
firm accepted some. She writes positive roles for women
in many of her books.

Jennifer Maiden 1949-

> The Terms (1982)

Poetry

> Tactics (1974)
> The Problem of Evil (1975)
> The Occupying Forces (1975)
> Birthstones (1978)
> The Border Loss (1979)
> For the Left Hand (1981)
> The Trust (1987)
> Winter Baby (1990*)

Poetry and Prose

> Mortal Details (1977)
> The Warm Thing (1983)

■Born in New South Wales. She left school early to work
in a factory. Returned to study and graduated in 1974.
Has worked as a tutor and editor and won several
awards.

Theresa Malkiel 1874-1949

> The Diary of a Shirtwaist Striker (1910)

■Born in Russia, she emigrated to the US. with her
family, in 1891 at the age of 17. She had begun to be
politically active in Russia, and continued this in New
York by being active in Trades' Union and women's
politics. She believed strongly that socialism and

feminism should be combined, and that women entering the workforce should fight for equality in terms of class and gender.

Ethel Mannin 1900-1984

> Martha (1923)
> The Late Miss Guthrie (1976)
> and fifty other novels.

■Born in London. Left school at 15 to work as a stenographer and later as a freelance writer. As a young adult she joined the ILP and declared herself an atheist, later she became an anarchist and pacifist. She lived and worked in different European countries. Her novels are socially and politically concious, often with a working-class woman as the central character. She also wrote seven books of autobiography from 1930 to 1971, travel books and children's books.

Jovette Marchessault 1938-

> Comme une enfant de la terre (1975)
> Tryptique Lesbienne (1980)
> Mere des herbes (1980)
> Des caillox blancs pour les forets obscures (1987)

Plays

> Vaches de Nuit (1979)
> Violette Leduc (1982)
> Alice et Gertrude (1984)

■Born in the Canadian countryside she was brought up in Montreal. She educated herself and worked in low-paid work as an encyclopaedia salesperson and in the textile industry. She travelled in Europe and uses her travels, work experience and Canadian Indian heritage in her writing.

Paule Marshall 1929-

Browngirl, Brownstones (1959*)
The Chosen Place, The Timeless People(1969)
Praisesong for the Widow (1983*)
Daughters (1993*)

Short stories

Soul Clap Hands and Sing (1961)
Reena (1983)
Merle: A Novella and other stories (1985*)

■Born in Brooklyn. Parents from Barbados. Mother a storyteller. Worked as a librarian, a journalist and as a teacher. Her stories describe the different pulls of being black in a white society, whether to try and integrate or to explore African roots.

Una Marson 1905-1965

Poetry

Tropic Reveries(1930, Institute of Jamaica medal)
Heights and Depths (1932)
The Moth and the Star (1937)
Towards the Stars (1945)

Plays

At What a Price (1932)
London Calling (1937)
Pocomania (1938)

■Born in Jamaica. Mother died young, which affected her greatly. Wrote poetry from young. Emigrated to Britain in 1936. Was active in different progressive movements, including for colonial independence, for Peace and for Britain's Black Theatre Company. Began and presented "Caribbean Voices" for BBC Radio. After the War, visited the US. continued to campaign and publish work.

Jill Miller No Dob.

>Happy as a Dead Cat (1983*)

History

>You Can't Kill the Spirit: Women in a Welsh Mining Valley (1986*).

■Left school at 15 with no formal qualifications. Both her books have been well received. She says of herself "Being brought up working-class, put a fire in my belly that can never be extinguished and a strong sense of the injustices of this world".

Anchee Min 1958-

Autobiography

>Red Azalea (1993*)
>Katherine (1995*)

■Born in Shanghai. Was a Red Guard from an early age. At the age of 17 she was sent to work on a collective farm. She was saved from this harsh life by being chosen as a film recruit for propoganda films in 1976. She was later dropped from the project and emigrated to the US. in 1984.

Oodgeroo Noonuccaal 1920-

Poetry

>We are Going (1964)
>The Dawn is at Hand (1966)
>My People (1970)

Short stories

>Stradbroke Dreamtime (1972)

■Born an Aborigine in Brisbane. Left school at 13 to work as a domestic. Largely self-educated. Served in Australian Women's Army, 1941-2. Worked in Aboriginal Rights' movement in the 60's and set up an educational centre in 1972. She assumed her current name in 1987 in protest at the continued ill-treatment of Aborigines, and uses her work to take the struggle for their rights to a wider audience.

Alice Notley 1945-

Poetry

165 Meeting House Lane (1971)

Waltzing Matilda (1981) and 11 others.

Autobiography

Tell Me Again (1982)

■Born in Arizona and brought up in California. Daughter of a garage mechanic. Of dual heritage, White/North American Indian. Bible-believing family background. Studied at University of Iowa and moved to New York. Her work mixes topical and personal issues.

Kate O'Brien 1897-1974

Without My Cloak (1931*)

The Ante Room (1934*)

Mary Lavalle (1936*)

Pray for the Wanderer (1938),

The Land of Spices (1941*)

Last of Summer (1943*)

That Lady (1946*)

The Flower of May (1953)

As Music and Splendour (1958)

Farewell Spain (Re-printed 1985*)

Homesick Garden (Re-printed 1992*)

Autobiography

Presentation Parlour (1956)

■Born in Limerick. Daughter of a horse-dealer who died when she was five. Went to convent school and then to university in Dublin. After leaving school worked as a reporter, teacher, secretary and governess in Spain. Ireland and Spain were the setting for most of her novels, often historical. Some of her books were banned at the time of publication. The author was successful early in life, but died in obscurity in Kent. Recently, she has had something of a revival and had her work reprinted with introductions. She also wrote travel books, plays, diaries and biography.

Gilda O'Neill 1951-

The Cockney Girl (1992*)
Whitechapel Girl (1993*)
The Bells of Bow (1994*)
Just Around the Corner (1995*)
Cissie Flowers (Due 1996)

Non-fiction

Pull No More Bines - An Oral History of East London Women Hop-Pickers (1990*)
A Night Out With the Girls - Women Having a Good Time (1993)

■Born in Bethnal Green and brought up in Bow. Family later moved to Dagenham. Authour passed 11+ but didn't feel she fitted into the system, because of class, and dropped out at 15. Later went back to education as a mature student and now has three degrees. Lives in Essex.

Tillie Olsen 1913-

Yonnondio (1932*)

Short stories

Tell me a Riddle (1961*)

Non-Fiction

Silences (1962*)

■Born in Nebraska. Daughter of a labourer, also secretary of the Nebraska Socialist Party. Parents fled Russia after Revolution failed in 1905. Family lived in poverty. Author left school young and continued to educate herself through public libraries. Joined the Young Communist League in 1930, aged 17. Wrote poems, a journal, skits and a musical. Was jailed for political activity in 1932. Married a printer and trade unionist in 1936 and did not write again until the 50's. Her work on class and gender have inspired a generation of scholars and writers. Her essays have been much anthologised.

Margaret Penn 1896-?

Autobiographical novels

>Manchester 14 Miles (1947*)
>The Foolish Virgin (1951*)
>Young Mrs. Burton (1954*)

■Born near Manchester to unmarried mother. Brought up by farm labourer and his wife as their own. Became a part-time domestic servant in 1909, while still at school. Later became a dressmaker and secretary and went to live with her natural family in London. Her first novel in particular is critically acclaimed for its historical accuracy.

Marge Piercy 1936-

>Going Down Fast (1969)
>Dance the Eagle to Sleep (1971)
>Woman on the Edge of Time (1976*)
>High Cost of Living (1978*)
>Vida (1980*)
>Braided Lives (1982)
>Fly Away Home (1984)
>Gone to Soldiers (1987)
>Small Changes (1987*)

Plays

>Last White Class (1982*)
>(with husband Ira Wood)

Poetry

>Breaking Camp (1968)
>Hard Loving (1969)
>Living in the Open (1976)
>The Twelve Spoked Wheel Flashing (1978)
>The Moon is Always Female (1980)
>My Mother's Body (1985*)
>Available Light (1988*)
>Summer People (1990*)
>Body of Glass (1993*)

3 Degrees Below Desperate (1994*)
Stone, Paper, Knife (1993*)

■Born in Detroit. Went to university and travelled in Greece and France in the late 1950's and 60's. Became politically active and was gassed and beaten on demonstrations which affected her health. Her fictional work is frequently political.

Stef Pixner 1945-

Poetry
Sawdust and White Spirit (1985)
Truth Dare or Promise (1985, contributor)

■Born in London. She was brought up by her mother, a typist, her father having been killed in the war. Her mother was a communist and the author joined the Young Communist League in 1959 at the age of 14. Went to Leeds University. Worked as a gardener, waitress, lecturer and therapist. Her poetry is sharp and witty.

Dawn Powell 1897-1965

Whither (1924)
The Golden Spur (1962*) and 18 others.

Plays
Big Night (1933)
Jigsaw (1934)
Lady Comes Across (1934, a musical)

■Born in Ohio. Mother died young, moved a lot when young between different relatives, rural and urban working-class families. Her work is seen as a satire on the middle-classes, though she intended it as realism.

Marsha Prescod No DoB

Poetry
Land of Hope and Tory (1985)

■Born in London to West Indian immigrant parents who

had come to live and work in the 1950's. Was involved in the Brixton writers group "Black Ink" from 1980 and with the Brent Black Music Workshop.

Anne Ranansinghe 1925-

> Poems (1971)
> Against Eternity and Darkness (1985)
> and four others.

■Born in Essen, Germany. Left for Britain in 1939 at the age of 14, but most of her family died in concentration camps. Worked as a nurse and as a journalist. Married and emigrated to Sri Lanka in 1939. Began to write poetry in 1968. She has drawn parallels between the political situation in the Germany of her youth and the country in which she now resides.

Renee 1929-

Plays

> Setting the Table (1981)
> Secrets (1982)
> Dancing (1982)
> Groundwork (1982)
> Wednesday to Come (1985)
> Pass It On (1986)

Short stories

> Finding Ruth (1987)

■Born a Maori, in Napier, New Zealand. Daughter of a farm-worker, her father committed suicide when she was four. She left school at 12 to work at a woolen mill and then at book-binding. She married a shop-assistant in 1949 and had a succession if jobs. In the 60's she wrote a column and reviews. She gained a degree at the age of 38, her marriage broke up and she came out as a lesbian. It was at this time that she gave up her married name and was known only by her first name. Her plays often have all-women casts. "Wednesday to Come" is about class and poverty.

Naomi Replansky 1918-

Poetry

Ring Song (1952)
The Dangerous World (1988)

■Born to Jewish parents in the Bronx, where she has lived all her life. Began to write poetry at the age of ten, and was first published in a magazine at the age of 16. Went to the University of California and lived for two and a half years in France. Worked in a factory, office, as a translator and as a computer programmer. Her poems explore the Holocaust.

Lola Ridge 1873-1941

Poetry

The Ghetto (1918)
Sun-Up (1920)
Red Flag (1920)
Firehead (1929)
Dance of Fire (1935)

■Born in Dublin, an only child. Emigrated with her family to New Zealand in 1887 at the age of four. As an adult moved to Australia and, after the death of her mother, to San Francisco in 1907. She worked there as a factory-hand and as an artist's model. Her poems were naturalistic, and celebrated the working class, the newly emerging Soviet Union and Jewish immigrants. Worked as an editor and travelled to Mexico and the Near East in the 1930's.

Denise Riley 1948-

Poetry

Marxism for Infants (1977)
No Fee (1978, co-written with Wendy Mulford)
Some Poems (1982)
Dry Air (1985)

Truth Dare or Promise (1985, Contributor)
Am I That Name? (1987*)
Four Falling (1993*)
Mop, Mop Georgette (1993*)

■Born in Carlisle. Adoptive daughter of a clerical assistant and a ship-yard worker. Went to University, worked as a translator and was active politically in Women's movement and against the Vietnam War. Has contributed to Spare Rib and Feminist Review.

Mary Rinehart 1876-1958

The Circular Staircase (1908)
The Street of 7 Sisters (1914)
K (1915)
The Amazing Interlude (1918)
This Strange Adventure (1929)
The Swimming Pool (1952)
Man in Lower Ten (Re-issued 1993*)

Autobiography

My Life (1931)

■Born in Pennsylvania. Daughter of a sewing-machine salesman. Trained as a nurse, and began to write mysteries for magazines at the turn of the century. At the outbreak of World War 1 she was working as a war-correspondent and writing romances too. From 1910-1940 she wrote a humourous column for the Saturday Post on the adventures of "Tish", a single woman.

Kate Roberts 1891-1985

Tea in the Heather (1968)
The Living Sleep (1976)
Feet in Chains (1976)
Abandoned Lives (1990)

Short stories

A Summer Day and other stories (1946)
Two Old Men and other stories (1981)

Anthology

The World of Kate Roberts (1991)

■Kate Roberts wrote in Welsh. She lived and worked in the valleys of North Wales and it was there that she found the inspiration and material from which to write. She also wrote under the pen name of Catherine Williams.

Sonia Sanchez 1934-

Poetry

Homecoming (1969)
We are a BadDDD people (1970)
Love Poems (1973)
A Blues Book for Blue Black Magical Women (1974)
I've Been a Woman (1979)
Homegirls and Hand Grenades (1984*)
Under a Soprano Sky (1987)

Plays

The Bronx is Next (1968)
Sister Sonji (1969)
Uh Uh (1974)
Generations (1986*)

■Born in Birmingham, Alabama. Brought up by various relatives including her grandmother, a kitchen-help. An early experience of an aunt spitting in a racist bus driver's face radicalised her. She discovered black writers and read voraciously from her early 'teens. Went to University in New York in the mid '50's. Her written work mirrors her political journey, taking in such influences as Malcolm X, Harriet Tubman and the Nation of Islam (she was a member 1972-1976). Her poetry is sometimes gentler, more reflective and personal.

Peig Sayers 1873-1958
Autobiography
>Peig (1935*)

Short stories
>Tales (1939)
>Old Woman's Reflections (Re-issued 1978*)

■Born in Kerry, Eire. One of 13 surviving children, she went into service at 13. She had an arranged marriage and 10 children herself. She lived on an island and was known as the "Queen of the Storytellers". Her autobiography was dictated to her son in Gaelic who wrote it down. Likewise her "Tales" (375 stories and 40 songs). She saw great changes in her life-time and died in hospital on the mainland, a widow and her children having emigrated.

Olive Senior 1943-
Plays
>Down the Road Again (1968)
>Summer Lightening (1986*)
>Arrival of the Snake Woman (1989*)

■She was adopted at the age of four by urban relatives. She has worked as a journalist, in publishing, public relations, as a researcher and now as a full-time writer. Her work tracks the move from the oral tradition of her working-class origins to an educated middle-class written form.

Jan Shinebourne 1947-
>Rainsplitter in the Zodiac Garden (1977*)
>Timepiece (1986)
>The Last English Plantation (1988)

■Born in Guyana. Daughter of an indentured labourer. Emigrated to Britain in 1970. Has worked here as a reviewer, editor and reviewer. Her novels are set in Guyana and explore issues of race and class.

Louise Shore b. ?1930

Autobiography

　　　　Pure Running (1982*)

■Born in Jamaica the author came to Britain in the 1960's where she settled in Hackney. She worked as a receptionist, in a laundry and as a shop assistant before being persuaded to write her life story by attending reading and writing classes at Centerprise.

Penelope Shuttle 1947-

　　　　An Excusable Vengeance (1967)
　　　　All the Usual Hours of Sleeping (1969*)
　　　　Wailing Monkey Embracing a Tree (1974*)
　　　　Mirror of the Giant (1980*)

Poetry

　　　　Nostalgia Neurosis (1968)
　　　　Hermaphrodite Album (1973*, Co-authored
　　　　with husband Peter Redgrave)
　　　　Glass Cottage (1976*)
　　　　Adventures with my Horse (1979)
　　　　The Orchard Upstairs (1980*)
　　　　The Lion from Rio (1986*)
　　　　Taxing in the Rain (1992*)

■Born in Staines, Middlesex. Went to a secondary-modern school, and left to become a shorthand typist. She suffered from mental health problems in her youth, and suffered from agoraphobia, anorexia and had a breakdown at 19. Her later work explores the relationship between the sexes.

Louise Simeon 1968-

Poetry

　　　　Reflections (1983*)

■Lives in Brixton with three daughters. Her work details the struggle of life on the dole.

Agnes Smedley 1892-1950

Autobiograhical novel

> Daughter of Earth (1929*)

Biography

> The Great Road - The Life and Times of Zhu De (1956 published posthumously)

Short stories

> Cell Mates (1918)
> China Correspondent (1984*)

History

> Chinese Destinies (1933)
> China Fights Back (1938)
> Battle Hymn of China (1976*)

■Born in Missouri and brought up in Colorado. Daughter of a labourer. Education was patchy. Dismissed as a teacher for being a socialist from a school in Arizona in 1916. She moved to New York where she got involved with the nationalist movement of India. She was arrested for political activities in 1918. Emigrated to Germany in 1920 and set up Berlin's first birth-control clinic. Her novel was written when her relationship with an Indian revolutionary in exile finished. When it was published, the reviewer in "The Nation" magazine called it America's "first feminist-proletarian novel." From 1928-1941 she became well known as she travelled in China writing and working as a journalist for the Manchester Guardian. At one time she moved with the Red Army as it fought the Nationalist forces. She frequently wrote on the changes to working people's lives due to the struggle for power. She returned to the US. in 1941 but was exiled by McCarthy and died in England, while trying to return to China. Her ashes are buried in Beijing's Cemetery for Revolutionaries, a rare honour for a non-Chinese citizen.

Jo Spence 1934-1992

Autobiography
> Putting Myself in the Picture (1986*)
> Family Snaps:The Meaning of Domestic
> Photography (1991* Ed.with Pat Holland)
> Re-inventing the Family Album: Handbook of
> Photography for Women (with Nina Kellgren)

Also contributed to
> Guidelines Photography (1978*)
> Photography/Politics One (1986*)
> Photography/Politics Two (1986*)

■ Born in London. Left school at 13 and went to secretarial college for two years. Worked as a secretary until 1967, when she opened a commercial photography studio in Hampstead. In 1974 she co-founded Photography Workshop, which later combined with Half Moon Photography Workshop and produced the magazine "Camerawork". Worked with youth workers, students and teachers. Also worked at the BFI as a secretary at this time. Held first exhibition in 1973. Did extensive research in Europe in 1981, with partner Terry Dennet, and graduated in 1982 from the Polytechnic of Central London. In 1982 discovered she had breast cancer. For the last ten years of her life she fought the illness, and recorded the fight photographically.

Cath Staincliffe No DoB.

> Looking for Trouble (1994*)

■ Born in Bradford in the 50's now living in Manchester. Her "Sal Kilkenny" character juggles life as a Private Investigator with life as a single mother.

Joyce Storey ?1917-

Autobiography
> Our Joyce (1987*)
> Joyce's War (1990*)

Joyce's Dream (1995)

■Born and brought up in Bristol, the author's first book tells of her childhood, her illness with TB., work, romance and entertainment in the 30's. Her second book details her war work in Bristol and Grimsby.

Maud Sulter 1960-
Poetry
> As a Blackwoman (1985*)
> Zabat (1989)
> Necropolis (1990)

■Born in Glasgow. She was brought up by her white grandfather and black mother. As a student she became involved in politics and has continued to campaign partly through her writing, for example for equal rights for black people and against the anti-abortion bill.

She has written for "Spare Rib" and worked as a girls worker and currently as an artist.

Bobbi Sykes 1943-
Poetry
> Love Poems and other Revolutionary Actions (1979)

Autobiography
> Mum Shirl (1981)

Thesis
> Incentive, Achievement and Community (1986)

■Born an Aborigine in Queensland. Left school at 14, though much later studied in the US. Her writing is both personal and political, exploring the role of a black woman in a predominantly white, racist society.

Amy Tan 1952-
Novels
> The Joy Luck Club (1990*)
> The Kitchen God's Wife (1991*)

■Born in California. Daughter of Chinese immigrants. Worked as an administrator, reporter and editor. Her novels are about the Chinese/American community and their recent history and explore the theme of belonging/ unbelonging.

Elean Thomas 1947-
Last Room (1992*)
Poetry and Short stories
From the Life of a Woman (1986)

■Born in Jamaica. She went to school and university on the island. After leaving college she worked as a journalist, performance poet and for the Workers' Party. She has performed in the Caribbean and Eastern Europe.

Gladys Thomas 1935-
Poetry
Cry Rage (1972)
Exiles Within (1986, Contributor)
Short stories
The Wynberg 7 (1987)
Spotty Dog (1987*)
Plays
Now We Are Not Alone (1987)
David and Diane (1987)
Men Without Women (1987)
Avalon Court (1992*)
Children's stories
Children of the Crossroads (1986)

■Born in Cape Town, South Africa. Born of dual heritage, under apartheid. Left school after primary education to work in a garment factory. Her work has reflected and commented on the situation in Africa and as as well as winning prizes, has been banned. Her plays looked at the way apartheid changed personal relationships, her poems and children's stories recorded the flattening of her home and others at Crossways to build a white estate. She was named on the Kwanza honours list (Chicago) in 1980 for "writing under oppressive conditions." She visited the US. in 1983 and is a member of the United Women's Conference and South African Writers. She is currently writing her autobiography.

Joyce Thomas 1938-

> Marked by Fire (1982)
> Bright Shadow (1983)
> The Golden Pasture (1986)

Poetry

> Bittersweet (1973)
> Inside the Rainbow (1982)

■Born in Oklahoma. Daughter of a bricklayer. Mother was a storyteller and encouraged her to write. As a child she worked in the cotton fields, helped bring up younger siblings and attended frequent gospel meetings with her family, all of which influenced her writing. She got a degree at the age of 28 and has since taught in the US, Nigeria and Haiti. She explores the links between sexism and racism.

Clara Thompson c.1869-1949

Poetry

> Ethiope Lays (1900)
> Gleanings of Quiet Hours (1907)

■Born in Ohio. Daughter of former slaves. Received basic education at state school and was financially supported by her brother when her parents died. She explored black emancipation in her work, and wrote some poems in dialect.

Flora Thompson 1876-1947

Autobiographical fiction

> Larkrise to Candleford (1945*)
> Still Glides the Stream (1948*)
> Heatherley (1976*)

Poetry

> Bog-Myrtle and Peat (1921)

■Born in Oxfordshire. Daughter of a stone mason and a nursemaid. Left school at twelve to become post-office clerk. Read and wrote voraciously throughout her life despite early poverty and later disapproval by her husband. She wrote for magazines for many years until her famous books were published. They are in a mixture of genres and record a way of life now gone that the author lived through; the gradual mechanisation of rural communities and the coming of the industrial age.

Liz Thompson No DoB.

Biography

> Just a Cotchell (1987*)

■Born and brought up in Wapping, the author's book describes characters spanning a century of life in the Eas End of London. She also writes and performs poetry.

Priscilla Thompson 1871-1942

Poetry

> Songs from the Wayside (1908)
> A Garland of Poems (1926)

■Born in Ohio. Sister of Clara Thompson (cf). Her poems were more humourous than her sister's, but still political. She wrote some verse in dialect.

Sue Townsend 1945-

The Secret Diary of Adrian Mole
(1982*, adapted for stage and TV.)
Growing Pains (1984*)
True Confessions (1990*)
Re-building Coventry (1991*)
The Queen and I (1993* adapted for stage)

Plays

Womberang (1979*)
Bazaar and Rummage (1982*)
Groping for Words (1983*)
The Great Celestial Cow (1984)

■Born in Leicester. Left school at 15. Worked in many different jobs, including as a youth leader. Her work is often (but not always) humourous and she often comments on class. In "The Queen and I" this is as comedy, where the Royal Family are forced to live on a council estate after a revolution in Britain; in "Womberang" it is as serious comment when a young, working-class woman waits in an NHS. waiting room.

Miriam Waddington 1917-

Poetry

Green World (1945)
The Season's Lovers (1958)
The Glass Trumpet (1966)
Say Yes (1969)
Dream Telescope (1972)
The Visitants (1981)

■Born in Winnipeg. Daughter of Russian-Jewish immigrant parents. Her childhood home was a meeting place for people to come for political and intellectual discussion. Her first language was Yiddish, she began to write in English at the age of ten. Gained a degree in 1939 in Toronto and worked as a columnist, social-worker and teacher. She has received several awards.

Diane Wakorski 1937-

Poetry

More than 50 collections of verse, from
> Coins and Coffins (1962) to
> Emerald Ice (1988)

■Born in California. Daughter of a sailor. Left school because she became pregnant. This, and her next child born soon after, were given up for adoption. Paid for herself to go through college by working in a bookshop, during which she had another child. Later worked as a teacher. Her work is in the tradition of lyric poets such as Yeats and Stevens.

Alice Walker 1944-

> The Third Life of Grange Copeland (1970*)
> Meridian (1976*)
> The Colour Purple (1982*, Pulitzer
> prizewinner, the first by a black woman)
> The Temple of My Familiar (1989*)
> Possessing the Secret of Joy (1992*)

Poetry

> Once (1968*)
> Revolutionary Petunias (1973*)
> Goodnight Willie Lee (1979)
> Horses Make a Landscape Look More
> Beautiful (1984*)
> Her Blue Body (1991*)

Short stories

> In Love and Trouble (1973*)
> You can't keep a Good Woman Down (1981*)

Essays

> In Search of Our Mothers' Gardens (1983*)
> Living by the Word (1988*)

Biography

> Langston Hughes (1974)

■Born in Georgia. Daughter of share-croppers. Encouraged to write by her mother. Her first book of poems was published while at college, when her tutor showed it to a publisher. Her two early novels paint a bleak and angry picture of life for black people in the US. of the 1930's and 1960's respectively. "The Colour Purple" links the main protagonists to Africa through African-American missionaries (a theme taken up again in "Possessing the Secret of Joy"). "The Temple of My Familiar" seems to veer towards the Magic Realism of some Latin American authors, and its themes of myth, spirituality and nature are explored further in her later essays.

Michelene Wandor 1940-

Plays

> You Two can be Ticklish (1970)
> The Day After Yesterday (1972)
> Mal de Mer (1972)
> Spilt Milk (1973)
> Care and Control (1977)
> Aid Thy Neighbour (1978)
> Future Perfect (1981)

Poetry and stories

> Upbeat (1982*)
> Gardens of Eden (1984*)
> Guests in the Body (1986*)

■Born in London. Daughter of Russian-Jewish immigrants. Went to secondary modern school in Chingford, then university at Cambridge. Worked as an editor. Has been very active in the Women's Liberation movement. Much of her work explores women's issues, with some of her plays written specifically for women's theatre groups.

Ellen Wilkinson 1891-1947

Clash (1929*)
The Division Bell Mystery (1931)

Non-fiction

The Town that was Murdered: Jarrow (1939)
Why Fascism? (1934, with E. Conze)

■Born in Manchester. Daughter of cotton operatives. Won scholarships and went to Manchester University. Became a teacher and then a Labour Member of Parliament in 1924. She served in Atlee's post-war cabinet as Minister for Education 1945-1947.

Barbara Willard 1909-

Many books for children, including

The Iron Lily (1973*)
(Guardian Award winner)

■Born in Brighton, daughter of actors. Went to convent school. Left to become an actor. Also worked as a play-reader. Her adult work as well as some of her childrens work is historical in nature.

Jeanette Winterson 1959-

Oranges are not the Only Fruit (1985*)
(Whitbread Award, adapted for TV 1990)
Boating for Beginners (1985*)
The Passion (1987*)
(John Llewelyn Rhys Memorial Prize)
Sexing the Cherry (1989*)
Written on the Body (1992*)
Art and Lies (1994*)

Short stories

Passion Fruit (1986*)

Radio play

Static (1988* Young Playwrights Award)

Non Fiction

Fit for the Future (1986*)

■Born in Manchester. Adopted daughter of a factory worker. Went to grammar school. Brought up in an evangelical household, she was prepared to become a preacher until she had a lesbian relationship at the age of 15 and left home. Went to Further Education college and worked as an ice-cream seller, domestic and in a funeral parlour to finance her studies. Later, took a degree at Oxford and worked in publishing and the theatre. Her experiences were the meat for her humourous first novel. After her second novel, her work became more exploratory and fantastic.

Anzia Yezierska 1880-1970

> Hungry Hearts (1920)
> Salome of the Tenements (1922)
> Bread Givers (1925*)
> Arrogant Beggar (1927)
> All I Could Never Be (1932),
> Red Ribbon on a White Horse (1950),
> The Open Cage (1979)

■Born in Poland, to Jewish parents. Emigrated to the New York with her family in the 1890's. Worked in sweat shops in the Lower East Side, and studied English at evening classes. Began teacher's training in 1900. Wrote without the support of her family. Her theme was often working women and their struggles. She was courted by Hollywood after the success of her first book, but she chose to ignore this and continue to write novels.

Helen Yglesias 1915-

> Hoe She Died (1972)
> Family Feeling (1976)
> Starting: Early, Anew, Over and Late (1978)
> Sweetsir (1981)
> The Saviours (1987)

■Born in New York to Jewish parents. Left school at 16 and worked in a succession of manual jobs. Later worked for communist and socialist groups and became an editor. Her work draws on her family background and her political activity.

Rida Young 1875-1926

Plays
>Brown of Harvard (1906, filmed 1925)
>The Lottery Man (1909)
>Little Old New York (1920)

and many other comedies. Also songs.

■Born in Baltimore. Went to state school and college. Worked as an actor on leaving college. Her plays were very popular in their time.

Marya Zaturenska 1902-1982

Poetry
>Threshold and Hearth (1934)
>Cold Morning Sky (1937, Pulitzer Prize)
>The Listening Landscape (1941)
>Collected Poems (1965)
>The Hidden Waterfall (1974)

Biography
>Christina Rossetti (1949)

■Born in Kiev, Russia. Emigrated to the US. with her parents in 1909 at the age of 7. Left school at the age of 12 to work in a factory. Studied at evening classes and eventually managed to go to university. Worked as a feature writer and editor.

Bibliography

The Oxford Guide to British Women Writers; ed.
Joanne Shattock; OUP.; 1993.

The Feminist Companion to Literature in English; eds.
Virginia Blain; Patricia Clements; Isobel Grundy;
B.T. Batsford Ltd; 1990.

Dictionary of British Women Writers; ed. Janet Todd;
Routledge;1989.

Black Women Writers at Work; ed. Claudia Tate;
Continuum; 1985.

Towards Recognition of Working-Class Women Writers;
Mel Cherry; Working Press; 1994.

Working-class Novelists 1930-1950; Howard Slater;
Working Press; 1993.

Black Feminist Criticism; Barbara Christian; Pergamon
Press; 1986.

In Other Words; ed. Gail Chester and Sigrid Nielsen;
Hutchinson;1987.

Towards Recognition of Working-Class Women Writers

By Merylyn Cherry

Introduction

In the course of my degree studies it became apparent that there was little historical evidence of British working-class women writers. This led me to question whether such women actually wrote or whether it was the case that their writing was not deemed good enough for publication. Catherine Cookson, for example, is from a working-class background and very popular and yet receives little attention. So who decides what is good enough? The feminist movement and feminist literary criticism do not seem to recognise British working-class women either. Are their interests so dissimilar? Surely recognition of women's lives and experience extends to all women.

It was on this basis that I set out to find examples of working-class women's writing and, if possible, to investigate their reception by feminist critics and academics. By examining their texts I hope to illustrate that they have written something worthy of recognition, regardless of whether received opinion considers them good or bad examples of literature.

The first task of this study, however, is to establish a definition of 'working class', a term which did not come into use until the early nineteenth century. The Oxford English Dictionary's entry reads "The grade or grades of society comprising those who are employed to work for wages in manual or industrial occupations." Invariably poor and underprivileged these grades are often referred to as the proletariat or lower classes.

There are many references to 'working women' in literature but the criterion for inclusion in this study is women whose class is defined by their economic position, a position based not just on selling their manual labour, but on their standing within the family and that family's position within society. They must occupy a position of domestic worker within a family whose existence and quality of life is dependent upon its members being engaged in waged, usually manual and unskilled, work. This study is not about representations of working-class women in literature but about working-class women's representations of themselves and the society in which they lived.

My second task is to identify the emergence of British working-class women writers in the twentieth century. To do this one must look at the historical and sociological background of these women and assess their opportunities for their practical and psychological application to writing, their literacy and motivation.

Background

> "Women did not seek self-fulfilment at the expense of the family because they saw little distinction between their own good and that of their families. There was a very low level of self-awareness."
> Elizabeth Roberts, 1984, p203

This 'low-level of self-awareness' perceived of working-class women in the period up to 1940 must have played a large part in preventing them from writing about themselves and their lives. However, a brief look at the difficulties imposed by society should explain why their interests and motivation were directed elsewhere.

Processes of industrialisation and capitalism in the late eighteenth and throughout the nineteenth centuries led also to the creation of a strata of society which became known as the middle class or bourgeoisie. Its financial success and social elevation highlighted the position of the lower classes whose changing lifestyle, from a rural economy - within which they could be self sufficient, living off the land in close-knit communities - to an urbanised poverty, found them part of an uneducated and illiterate labour force in a strictly divided society. Defined by Marx as a proletariat exploited for profit, the working class became feared by the higher classes as the 'masses' who could easily become an unruly mob.

The Chartist movement and social reformers forced the government to consider the benefits of educating the nation's workforce. While the reformers looked to education as a solution to poverty, the state and the Church wished for a more God-fearing underclass who could be manipulated to behave in a more civilised manner. Andrew Ure, who wrote 'The Philosophy of Manufactures' in 1835, took for granted the virtues of the middle classes and regarded the working classes as an enemy who should not be educated above their station or expect any advancement through it. He believed that

> "The poor must be rescued from pauperism and subversion and trained to be docile and diligent workers. That is the primary purpose of education" (Tholfsen, 1976, p44).

By the middle of the nineteenth century, adult education had become popular amongst many working-class men who, with the backing of religious organisations and some employers, wished to improve themselves. Education had traditionally been the responsibility of the family and the Church but Forster's Elementary Education Act of 1870 made elementary schooling the responsibility of the state. The literacy rate was to shoot up from this time but in 1861 only 5% of all children remained at school after eleven years old and this was to remain little changed until the First World War (Heyck, 1982, p25). Many children were allowed out of school to help their mothers on laundry days or after confinements etc.

It became acceptable for some children to be 'half-timers' - at work and school. Once they left school their family became so dependent on their meagre wages that few had the strength of mind, energy, or opportunity to further their education. However, Mechanics Institutes had libraries for their workers and some tobacco shops and stationers had small lending libraries, but these remained the domain of men. Industrial demand had meant that one third of women with children under eleven went to work (and this did not include the wives who worked at home helping their husbands - shoemakers, innkeepers, farmers etc.) (Foster, 1974, p96). Working-class conditions at home and work were appalling and women in particular, with no relief from household chores, had little or no opportunity to read or write.

The lifestyles of working-class women bore little relationship to the middle-class ideology of women as the 'angel in the house'. However, a remnant of this notion, that a woman's place was in the home, and the practical need for domestic labour meant that domestic work became encoded in state education. Plain needlework for girls had been compulsory since the Education Code of 1862 and the new Education Code of 1876 meant that every girl must take domestic economy; in 1882 there were grants for practical teaching of cookery and in 1890 for laundry work, (Roberts, 1984, p30). A Board School Inspector, Mrs. Marvin, did feel that a liberal education was more important "to raise the woman's status, to elevate her character, and to widen her intellectual outlook" (Dyhouse, 1981, p170) but many other middle-class women were elitist. Clara Collett, in her address to the Bryce Commission on Secondary Education in 1894, maintained that academic scholarships were not suitable for working-class girls because they raised a girl's aspirations unrealistically when they might have to content themselves with a job as a post office clerk or a shop assistant, (ibid, p171). Such education as was available was seen as necessary to produce good wives and mothers for the character of a mother was considered important in assuring the worth of children. It followed social trends in that it contributed towards the needs of the middle and upper classes who found it difficult to get good domestic help. Carol Dyhouse (1981, Chapter 3, p79) claims that school needlework answered the need for mending for the squire's household in rural areas and that plain cooking and nutrition were important in urban areas when recruits for the Boer War were found to be unfit for active service. Infant mortality rates "couched in the rhetoric of the 'national efficiency debate'" were blamed on the ignorance of mothers, (ibid, p95) and many of the 'faults' of society were laid at their door.

Dyhouse cites Samuel Smiles saying of woman in 1843 that "the performance of domestic duties is her proper office" and, thirty years later, "women can no more do men's special work in the world than men can do women's. And whenever woman has withdrawn from her home and family to enter upon other work, the result has been socially disastrous" (1981, p80). Employment in domestic work, however, was not popular with women. It involved 'living-in', long hours and low pay. Most preferred to work outside the home-environment and factory work provided an element of autonomy. Girls would learn how to handle their own money and mix with a wide range of people. Inevitably factory life was considered a bad influence and girls clubs were introduced such as the Girl Guides and Friendly Societies in an attempt to "raise the slum girl from the gutter" (ibid, p110). The 'Snowdrop Bands' were dedicated to preserving purity amongst working girls and each member carried a card with a promise written on the back "...we will, with God's help, earnestly try, both by our example and influence to discourage all wrong conversation, light and immodest conduct and the reading of bad and foolish books" (cited Dyhouse, 1981, p109). Reading was considered dangerous for girls and working women's autobiographies reveal that employers thought it would interfere with their work, which consequently jeopardised their jobs. "Because of the sexual division of labour reading and writing threatened rather than advanced women's work" (Gagnier, 1989, p40).

With the increase of literacy came a demand for literature. One of the biggest developments in the nineteenth century was a mass readership of the radical press and a new tradition of 'collective class expression':

> "There was one peculiar fact which could not but strike every reflecting person at the present day, and that was the number of writers springing up among the working classes... They had in them the rich racy spirit of our old English writers... when the whole of this literature was considered it would be found pervaded by a spirit of indignation which would arise among men who felt themselves reduced to a slave class."
> (W.J.Fox M.P. 1847 cited Foster, 1974, p147)

A new militancy had developed amongst working men and women in industry that saw the publication of political tracts and essays. A genuine working-class tradition is to be found in Chartist verse, some regional poets and in the memoirs of working men who rose to eminent positions in public life. T.W.Heyck claims that this led to a greater fear of the masses by the bourgeoisie that expressed itself in the imposition of a stamp tax to make "dangerous working-class literature" too expensive for its market (1982, p27).

At the same time middle-class writers were showing an awareness of working-class conditions, and books about them, by authors such as Charles Dickens and Elizabeth Gaskell, became popular. Some writers such as Constance Howell and Margaret Harkness supported

Chartism and Socialism and were "committed to a working-class point of view" but amongst popular middle-class literature a more romantic approach prevailed (Keating, 1971, p240). Keating maintains that a fictional working-class family evolved, often comprising a brutal stepfather, gentle religious mother, selfish sisters etc. Romantic working-class heroes are often found to have secret upper-class backgrounds. The majority of middle-class novelists stopped short on the threshold of describing real working-class life due to their lack of real experience or knowledge of such things.

Whilst working-class men were struggling for recognition, equality and justice within society, middle-class women were actively struggling against a sexual division of labour which kept them economically dependent on men. Education for middle-class women was designed to make them better wives and mothers, "better companions for men" (Dyhouse, 1981, p140). It taught bourgeois women femininity and the idea that their sole aim in life was to be 'the angel in the house'. Women began to rebel against what Olive Schreiner described as this 'parasitism' and demanded the same education as men; the same curricula and examinations. They recognised that the sexual division of labour tied them to low paid jobs, usually unskilled and of low status. Whilst working-class women became sweated labour and domestic skivvies, middle-class women had become unpaid 'household managers'. A cultural ideology which professionalised middle-class men's employment and placed it in the abstract world of mental work meant that all women were relegated to a practical role which required no intellectual exercise. They were, therefore, psychologically and socially excluded from the mental task of writing as a paid occupation. (See Gagnier, 1989, pp38-40)

At the turn of the century the 'new women', middle-class rebels of the era, were articulating a feminist rhetoric which expressed itself in the suffrage movement. Proletarian women, however, despite their role in the industrial workplace found no voice in the emergent trade unions and only a very few became suffragettes. The Women's Co-operative Guild was able to offer an outlet for working-class women to articulate their lives in service of political projects and some also contributed short stories to the Co-operative Movement's publications but theirs was not consciously in the feminist cause. They were more concerned with the physical conditions of their lives than with competing with men of their class.

Crucially, if working-class women were conscious of their exploitation they interpreted it in terms of class conflict and did not consider themselves any more oppressed than their husbands. Feminism, in the sense of patriarchal domination, was not an immediate issue. Elizabeth Robert's study of working-class women in Lancashire shows that their lives' chief preoccupation was with the struggle against poverty.

> "In their interviews many women indicated their awareness of the limited horizons and opportunities of their lives, but were just as likely to associate their menfolk with this lack of choice." (1984, p2).

They saw themselves and their menfolk as being oppressed by their employers and the rich and middle classes generally. In addition to poverty, the stress in their lives could be compounded by illness, death, unemployment, migration and drunkenness.

Under such conditions women developed a strong network and support system in which extended families and a sense of community were vital. In many working-class areas women were central to the well-being of the family. The husbands provided and the women managed. Wives were seen as responsible for domestic matters and for moral standards which hinged on fundamental beliefs. These were concerned with being a 'good

Christian' and loving thy neighbour and involved a strong sense of justice with punishment for sin. The capitalist system, however, had imbued them primarily with a work ethic. Hard work was not only necessary to survival - young workers' wages were essential to the family and often they had no financial independence until marriage - but had intrinsic moral value.

The majority of girls became domestic servants, shop assistants or factory workers, usually in the textile industry, and the universal assumption was that they would marry within ten years of leaving school.

> "In the majority of working-class marriages it would appear to be misleading and inaccurate to see the wife as downtrodden, bullied and dependent. She was much more likely to be respected and highly regarded, financial and household manager, and the arbiter of familial and indeed neighbourhood standards." (Roberts, 1984, p124)

It is against this background of a society in which middle-class women were a useful and yet mainly decorative appendage to their husbands whilst working-class women, who toiled from morning to night with little or no leisure time, were vital to the survival of their families and the country's economy, that we come to examine some of the very few examples of working-class women's writing

The Writers

> "I have heard it said that working people are not worth writing about because they have few refinements of perception, that lack of intelligence denies them expression, and people who can't express themselves are not good material for the novelist. This may be so if the novelist has neither sympathy nor imagination." Alan Sillitoe (Tressel, 1986, p.9)

It has been very difficult to establish a tradition or canon of working-class women writers for this dissertation and the restricted availability of these writers' books, together with an absence of any significant critical acclaim or comment, was another stumbling block to the depth of this research. I hesitate to use the words 'tradition' and 'canon' for such writers because I rebel against these ideas as elitist and exclusive, but within the literary establishment it would seem a necessary qualification to categorise these women if they are to be acknowledged and acclaimed. Officially there does not seem to be a suitable category for them although the work of twentieth-century working-class male writers has become a recognised area within English literature today. Historians and critics have identified working women's writing going back to the sixteenth century but invariably these were relatively educated women whose social status had been lowered by reduced circumstances. There has been a tendency to bracket 'working women' with working-class men as marginal to literary consideration. It would seem consequently that working-class women are so marginalised as to be out of sight. However, more recent Victorian examples of purely autobiographical accounts of hard working-class lives have been recorded. (See Swindells, 1985, pp117-135)

The notion that literature has been constructed with middle-class values and ideologies is frequently underlined. Gagnier states that "individualist aesthetics have been used to disqualify women's and worker's lifewriting" (1989 p36), so how does one identify women writers for the purpose of this study? Rebecca O'Rourke provided a starting point with her essay 'Were There No Women?' in which she writes of a period starting with the years of economic depression in the 1920s and 1930s. She believes that the endurance of the novel on private and public bookshelves, although a bourgeois form of literature, has enabled working-class expression to exist.

She identifies "those rare writers of novels - Ethel Mannin, Kate Roberts, Margaret Penn, Flora Thompson" (O'Rourke, 1988 p51) - whose books, with the exception of Flora Thompson's work, 'Lark Rise to Candleford', are no longer in print. Their books are more likely to be in second-hand bookshops or in reserve stock than on library shelves. Add to these names Ethel Carnie, an early Trade Unionist, Ellen Wilkinson, a Labour M.P., and later writers such as Jessie Kesson and Catherine Cookson and we have representatives of fifty years of little acknowledged working-class women's writing.[1] (Despite her relative fame and popularity, Cookson has not generally been considered worthy of inclusion in academic literary criticism.)

Although writing in the accepted genre of the novel these writers are concerned to write themselves, their history and their experience into their texts. Indeed, Margaret Penn's and Flora Thompson's novels are largely autobiographical and greatly valued for their contribution to history and sociology. The literary establishment has relegated Catherine Cookson to the area of popular romantic fiction but she is no less valuable in her vivid descriptions of working-class life. Most of these women showed an ability or an interest and desire to write at an early age but only Mannin and Carnie were published before they were thirty years old. Carnie and Wilkinson were politically motivated and wished to offer a socialist polemic through fiction. For Cookson and Thompson the opportunity to write did not present itself until later in life. Flora Thompson had to raise her children and cope with the hostility to writing from her husband and his family before her novel was published when she was sixty-three years old. Catherine Cookson worked at menial jobs before becoming a laundry manageress and did not start writing until her marriage to a headmaster at the age of forty. Like Cookson, Jessie Kesson was illegitimate, had mental health problems and worked in unskilled jobs before her work was first published when she was forty-three years old.

The nature of the writers' lives, their texts and their gender, of course, would make it pertinent to apply the critical techniques of Marxism and Feminism when studying their work. Marxism, because I shall approach the texts from a class-conscious perspective, looking at the economic and environmental factors influencing the production of the novels, and feminism because I am consciously and, no doubt, subconsciously offering a specifically female and feminist reading of women's texts. I am seeking to rediscover an area of writing that has been ignored. Marxist criticism seeks to locate the author and her subject in the context of her society and the literary means of production. It would see the text constructed and restricted by a bourgeois ideology designed to reinforce capitalism and maintain the status quo. Before the Second World War this would have been seen in physical terms in which the ruling classes, in their efforts to extract profit from labour, would have kept the potential author so busy with, and dependent on, hard physical labour that she would have no opportunity to write. Marxists identify canons of literature as being socially evaluated and their criticism can be seen as valuing those texts which recognise economic oppression and highlight the political struggle for a classless society. It has been suggested that Ethel Mannin did not receive the critical attention that she deserved because of her "radical politics, highly individualised manner, and working-class status" (Schlueter, 1988 p310). She was an atheist and member of the Independent Labour Party in the 1930s (later becoming an anarchist and pacifist), was politically aware of the role of class and gender within society, and is quoted as having said "I am one of those who believe that the writer should concern himself with current affairs, be of his time, concerned with its problems, social and political" (Schlueter, 1988 p310). She recognised women's oppression and in her polemic 'Women and the Revolution', (1938), she argued that "feminist aims will be met by the post-revolutionary classless society" (Blain et al,1990 p709). Marxist Feminists make a direct connection between capitalism and the oppression of women. They feel that socioeconomic realities are fundamental to women's oppression, that capitalism is an effect of patriarchy which displaces "the question of women's subordination through the sexual division of labour under different modes of production" (Cora Kaplan in Eagleton, 1991 p161).

The ethos of feminist criticism has been to recognise the existence of women writers and to value their experience. Feminist criticism argues that, due to patriarchy, women's texts have had to be placed within the context of a male dominated society and therefore we must strive to identify women's specificity, women's experience and their contribution to literature. Within this theory, one icon has been Virginia Woolf who was writing at the same time as Carnie and Mannin. She became part of an elite literary set who adopted modernism as their trademark. As an answer to her struggle for recognition, Woolf wished to establish a female aesthetic in order to affirm women's writing. In doing this she believed that androgyny could express both masculinity and femininity - "femaleness and maleness, nurturance and aggression" (Eagleton, 1991 p25). Mary Eagleton states that Woolf betrayed her literary genius by "her adoption of a female aesthetic that ultimately proved inadequate to her purposes and stifling to her development" (ibid) and yet, it must be argued, this was the only way she could assert herself in the literary world. Working-class writers, in the meantime, who used realism as the only tool with which to portray the lives of the majority of the population, to be read by far more people and therefore contemptuously called 'popular', received little or no critical attention.

Self-writing

> "We eat, we sleep, we work, endlessly work from Monday morning to Saturday night, without remission. Cultivation of the mind? How is it possible? Reading? Those of us who are determined to live like human beings and require food for mind as well as body, are obliged to take which time is necessary for sleep to gratify this desire." (A Crewe Factory Girl 1894, cited in Nield Chew, 1982, p13)

Lack of information about working-class women writers has meant that what research is available has been largely confined to autobiography or self-writing, or at least this is where academia chooses to site it. Brian Maidment, in his study of Victorian artisan poetry which he acknowledges found no substantial body of women writers, feels that in previous studies of working-class writing, "the emphasis has fallen heavily on Chartist writing, on local writing, especially in dialect, and on the genre of autobiography, in fact the only literary genre other than poetry much used by self-taught writers," (Maidment, 1987, p16).

Maidment prefers the term 'self-taught' to 'working class' thus inferring the generally held view that working-class writing is different and in some way inferior, and illustrates how autobiography as a genre is given short shrift by the literary establishment. This is a double-edged sword for, as Wendy Webster notes, autobioigraphy has been the major genre in which working-class women have written, or at least the only genre in which their efforts have been recognised, and at the same time seen as the only genre appropriate for them. "It occupies a low place in the hierarchy of genres, so that it offered working-class women a form which did not involve claims to high artistic aspiration," (Bonner et al, 1992, p1).

One-off accounts of hard-working lives have been discovered and are valuable to historians but they also raise the issue of such women's motivation and opportunity to write. When it occured to poor women to write it would have been a personal outlet or forum possibly only intended for family and friends to read, if an intention to be read was there at all. Flora Thompson's letters from her mother:-

> "followed the home news and news of the neighbours, all told in simple, homely language, but with the tang of wit and occasional spice of malice which made her conversation so racy. She always wrote four or five pages and often ended her letters with 'My pen has run away with me again,' but there never was a word too much for Laura [Flora]. She kept her mother's letters to her for years and afterwards wished she had kept them longer. They deserved a wider public than one young daughter." (Thompson, 1973, p.496)

As 'The Autobiography of the Working Class' notes in its introduction - "The most obvious distortion in the body of autobiographies is the small number written by women...Little can be explained in terms of inequalities in elementary education or basic literacy...A more likely reason is the low status and self confidence of women in this period, and in particular their exclusion from most collective working-class activity." (Burnett et al, 1984, p.xviii).

All the writers in this study initially wrote for pleasure as children and needed encouragement or recognition to pursue authorial intent any further. Flora Thompson is quoted as saying, "To be born in poverty is a terrible handicap to a writer. I often say to myself that it has taken one lifetime for me to prepare to make a start." (cited O'Rourke, 1988, p58).

Working-class writers were very much on their own and had to break away from the restrictions of their class or background in order to write. It is significant that neither Flora Thompson or Ethel Mannin were forced into domestic service or factory labour when they reached an age of employment. Flora was placed as a junior assistant to a post mistress and Ethel became a stenographer. In the case of Ethel Carnie and Catherine Cookson it was marriage that actually liberated them to write; the release from the need of paid employment to survive gave them their space. Conversely, Flora Thompson's husband and his family were against her writing but she wrote short stories and verse in order to pay for her children's education. Ethel Mannin wrote novelettes whilst she was pregnant and, after the breakdown of her marriage, went on to write professionally.

Rarely has it been acknowledged that story telling was a natural art of working women. Too busy to read if literate, gossip and story telling were a vital part of women's education and communication. Nursery rhymes and cautionary tales were handed down from mother to daughter, from older sister to younger sibling, from nursery maid to child etc.

"Laura and her brother would watch Queenie, the lacemaker and loved to see the bobbins tossed hither and thither, at random it seemed to them, every bobbin weighted with its bunch of bright beads and every bunch with its own story, which they had heard so many times that they knew it by heart, how this bunch had been part of a blue bead necklace worn by her little sister who had died at five years old, and this other one had belonged to her mother, and that black one had been found, after she was dead, in a work-box belonging to a woman who was reputed to have been a witch. [Queenie, in her childhood, had been 'brought up to the pillow'] - sitting among the women at eight years old and learning to fling her bobbins with the best of them. They would gather in one cottage in winter for warmth, she said, each one bringing her faggot or shovel of coals for the fire, and there they would sit all day working, gossiping, singing old songs, and telling old tales till it was time to run home and put on the pots for their husbands' suppers." (Thompson, 1973, p.83)

The stories of women told in autobiography give a vivid picture of everyday lives and emotions and in this Flora Thompson was especially gifted. Beautifully written and most readable Thompson's 'Larkrise to Candleford', 1948, has achieved the status of a minor classic. Written in the third person, although essentially autobiographical, it charts 'Laura's' early life in the hamlet of Lark Rise to her first employment with the postmistress of Candleford. It is highly valued as an historical record of the transition from rural life to that of an urban community but as a piece of literature it has received little attention. One exception is a critique by Juliet Dusinberre who praises Thompson's ability to remove the barrier of age and allow the reader to see the village life through a child's eye. Thompson does not thrust Laura forward as the heroine of the story but allows her to remain on the periphery as an observer and by using the 'child's eye and the adult's voice' "everywhere demonstrates the power and fascination of a story, and this is where the child nudges away the cool recording adult" (Dusinberre, 1984, p.63)

However, Webster claims that working-class women wrote autobiographies as a record of a way of life, as something that was of historical interest, because it was the only way they could justify writing about themselves, who they perceived to be of no interest as individuals. In today's climate of feminist criticism this could not be further from the truth. Many feminist writers feel that it is essential to rediscover individuals women's lives and highlight the need to reconstitute memory in order break the silence of women's history and promote the women's movement. "It is rather the case that a movement which has been one of the powerless, depending on oral rather than written words, on lived culture rather than text, is in constant danger of losing its memory." (Swindells, 1985, p.120).

Margaret Penn's novel 'Manchester Fourteen Miles' received enthusiastic reviews when it was published in 1947. Regarded as fiction based on fact, its autobiographical nature was ignored. John Betjemen declared "I have read much North Country rough stuff, realistic novels smelling of drains and sweat - and thick with local accents written, alas, phonetically. I think 'Manchester Fourteen Miles' by Margaret Penn is worth the lot of them." (Penn, 1979, p.xii). It was only when she was in her eighties that Margaret Penn confirmed that the story was autobiographical and that only the names had been changed. The 1976 edition is, in fact, accompanied by family photographs. The introduction by John Burnett belatedly recognises its contribution to literature and history and praises Penn for her success in writing an interesting account of 'ordinary life'. She "succeeds in doing so brilliantly, with accomplished style, humour, and a detachment which reveals her own faults and virtues as fully and intimately as those of her supporting cast" (ibid p.xi).

A characteristic of men's autobiography has been the theme of social and economic advancement, a chronological narrative with some heroic achievement. In working-class men's self-writing the emphasis has been less on the individual and more on a class-conscious awareness of their social group. Julia Swindells claims that "In reading women's experiences in autobiographical form, the formula of self advancement and of subjectivity, their relation to the genre is more complicated again" (ibid, p.139). She feels that for working women, more especially in the nineteenth century, models of social advancement rarely existed. For Margaret Penn writing of her childhood in the early twentieth century, advancement to higher social standing, although still within working-class levels, is a central issue. An avid reader, the central character, Hilda Winstanley, continually strives for more books and information and soon becomes aware of the deprivations of her family and the relative privileges of others. Her foster mother, Lizzie Winstanley, "was afraid of newspapers. She said they boded no good for them that read them, and she was firmly convinced that they were written by t'Owd Lad [the Devil] himself." (Penn, 1976, p.13). She had a similar view of Hilda reading novelettes, "Put it away, our 'ilda. No good will come of reading such wickedness." (ibid, p.17) Both her foster parents were illiterate and Lizzie, especially, had a deep fear and suspicion of the written word. For Hilda, literature revealed another world and was the source of much self-education, but reading was considered synonymous with high aspirations and "some day she'd have to earn her keep same as everybody else, and what good then would all this book-reading be to her?" (ibid, p.20)

Hilda's life is dominated by school and Chapel. Both are sources of literature, for book prizes are awarded for good conduct and achievement. The rivalry between Church and Chapel illustrates the local hierarchy, and it is as a part-time servant at the vicarage that Hilda learns social skills and "the quiet, unhurried routine of the gentry's way of life...Until she went to the Vicarage, Hilda had never seen an indoor closet: it was a luxury and a mark of gentility which made a greater impression upon her than all the other refinements put together" (ibid, pp

203-4).Most importantly, however, the 9d a week wages enabled her to pay 2d a week to use the Co-op library.

Swindells sees irony in the fact that working women's desire for education did not further them in the patriarchal system of society, they were no less oppressed.

> "That most of the women autobiographers retain an attachment to books and to knowledge as crucial aspects of autobiographical self-perception is a testament to the power of the illusion of the possibility of change through learning, but it is also a testament to acts of daring in the teeth of the pressures of conformism." (Swindells, 1985, p.132)

In retrospect we can look at these women's lives and see that this is so. But to most women patriarchal oppression was not part of their consciousness. To rise above domestic service was an achievement in itself, and through this the opportunity to marry slightly above one's station was progress enough. These autobiographical novels clearly show the problems faced by girls if they wished to break the mould of domestic and factory work and branch out into other areas of employment. For work they must. "And to be self-supporting...was surely the aim of any right-thinking, well brought-up girl" as young Hilda is told as she approaches her thirteenth birthday (Penn, 1976, p.200).

Working-class girls expectations fell far short of Virginia Woolf's aim of 'a room of one's own and £500 per year'. Swindells, in her studies of working women's writing in the nineteenth century, was concerned about the exclusion of women from professions and sought to find some writing that would challenge dominant forms of representation. She hoped to find this in working-class autobiographies but found that they had been "strongly mediated by twentieth century social historians" who allowed no sense of the fact that "the texts themselves are imaginative constructions with their own biases and partialities," (Swindells, 1985, p118).

The fact that working-class women's self-writing is placed in the context of social history rather than literature is just one of the reasons that impede the recognition of working-class women writers. Lack of confidence may have induced them to write in the third person or, perhaps, an awareness that market forces would promote a novel rather than an autobiography but, as Margaret Penn and Flora Thompson so adequately illustrate, autobiography is not an inferior genre but a skilled and entertaining literary art form which is not beyond the mastery of working-class women. Scholes & Kellogg say in 'The Nature of Narrative' that

> "If any distinction can be said to exist between autobiography and the autobiographical novel it resides not in their respective fidelity to facts but rather in their respective originality in perceiving and telling the facts. It is in the knowing and telling, not in the facts that art is to be found." (cited Lodge, 1971, p 126)

I admit that lack of working-class novelists led me to include autobiographical novels in this study but they are by no means less 'literary' than fiction. All realist novels are informed by the writer's experience and the books by Penn and Thompson are interesting, entertaining and readable and deserve literary attention.

Socialism and Style

> "All those questions, I found myself thinking, which matter so intensely to people here, questions of sanitation and education and wages, this demand for an extra shilling, or another year at school, for eight hours instead of nine behind a counter or in a mine, leave me, in my blood and bones, untouched." Virginia Woolf, 1930 (cited in Freeman, 1985, p37)

Thus Virginia Woolf's memories of a meeting of the Women's Co-Operative Guild epitomised the attitude of many people to the concerns of the working class. This was despite changes in social and aesthetic attitudes which enabled writers to question the establishment and speak of the injustices inflicted on the poor so that "from being problematic, dangerous, threatening, the working classes now emerge as valiant, exploited, victimised" (Eagleton & Pierce, 1979, p69). Literary criticism has eventually given credence to working-class writers (although these are inevitably men) and critical studies of their work have identified certain traits and characteristics which have linked working-class writing to social conditions and political struggle.

The relationship between realism and working-class writing has also been taken for granted. The concern of the writers to portray common experiences, the sense of community and environment, of life and death within families and the struggle against poverty, all ingredients in working-class women's writing, became an aesthetic ideology. The working classes are depicted as bound within the social framework and stereotypical images emerge. Some critics see the danger of this ideology becoming a 'sentimental populism' which implies a preconception of working lives and behaviour, (see Davies, 1984, p125). This may be one of the reasons why working-class women's writing was not and is not taken seriously in more influential literary circles.

Some male working-class writers were seen as men with a message and those texts with a strong political content are labelled as 'socialist novels' by writers such as H. Gustav Klaus who defines them as being "written in the historical interests of the working class" (Klaus, 1985, p108). He claims that the socialist novel matured with writers such as Robert Tressel and developed "almost from the outset, by downgrading the role of the central individual hero. Instead of presenting unique individuals in extraordinary circumstances, the socialist novel tends to emphasise the representativeness of its characters and the commonness of their position" (ibid, p126).

Ethel Carnie is the only working-class woman identified as a socialist novelist by writers like Klaus and P.M. Ashraf and yet her books, which were very popular in the North of England in the early decades of this century were not overtly political. Despite her involvement with the socialist movement and labour journalism she did not take up specific incidents or political causes as central issues in her novels. Her success lay in the authentic portrayal of individual women as they struggled to cope with the poverty and hard facts of their existence, whether at home or work, Socialist convictions were portrayed as natural expressions in their way of life. Carnie's natural realism meant that "the emotional frustration or the social and economic inequality of women are not often in the consciousness of her characters, although present in their whole position. They may instinctively revolt against being treated as inferiors, or a slight incident makes the point. The trade union official leaves the meeting in his car, while the woman speaker has to walk to the station." (Ashraf, 1979,p177)

Carnie's first novel, 'Miss Nobody', 1913, features a heroine, Carrie, who marries 'sensibly' for financial security but in the course of the story finds that she must learn to stand alone. She leaves home and finds work in Manchester as a flax mill hand but eventually gets boycotted for instigating a successful strike for a pay rise. She does not return to her husband until he is in trouble and needs her, and only then do they find happiness together. Without writing a didactic socialist novel in which the heroine's response to capitalist tyranny is the central point of the story, Carnie succeeds in showing an unstereotypical heroine who rises to the challenges of life in a sympathetic and humane way. Struggling against the wind Carrie and a workmate "clung together against the wall of a house, laughing because it was just as easy to laugh as cry, and because there is grim humour in fighting against things and getting the best of them, to the working-class mind." (Carnie, 1913, p153).

Her modest acclaim as a socialist novelist lies in her success in portraying a thought-provoking story as a piece of popular fiction that would be read and enjoyed by many people without alienating them by the use of serious socialist propoganda.

Klaus considers that many novelists have a problem relating "the central fact of class struggle to the lives of individuals," (Klaus, 1986, p93). Carnie overcomes this by foregrounding the lives of particular women whose very existence is dictated by their class status. Ellen Wilkinson's novel 'Clash', however, is criticised for focussing on the "higher reaches of the trade union hierarchy instead of the activities of the rank and file" (ibid, p93). Ellen Wilkinson was a Labour M.P. with a working-class background whose novel, although interweaving human stories, was centred on the General Strike of 1926. Left-wing people of prominence were at pains to allay fears of communism and promote the rejection of violence. The problem of revolution and the relationship between classes was "one of the dominant themes of the few fictional expressions of socialist propoganda during this period" and a common device was for the hero or heroine to convert to socialism through romance (Smith, 1978, p41). Unfortunately, as in 'Clash', the heroine rarely finds love outside her own class but the more pragmatic objectives of socialist polemic novels were for the right to work, a minimum wage and an eight hour day.

Ethel Mannin, like Carnie, was a socialist and she successfully sites men and women in the capitalist order and O'Rourke describes some of her novels, e.g. 'Cactus', 1935, and 'Ragged Banners', 1935, as "socialist epics", (O'Rourke, 1988, p58). In her third novel, 'Sounding Brass', 1925, "a satire on the advertising world in which I served my apprenticeship" (Mannin, 1974, pp2842) and which established her as a novelist, she charts the career of James Rickard, publicist and businessman. At an early age Rickard becomes fascinated with the power of money and, indifferent to fellow human beings, proceeds to use and dismiss people, especially women, in order to get on. A collier's son, Rickard leaves school at fourteen but, refusing to follow his father down the pit "like a rat in a hole", he robs his dying grandmother and makes his way to London where he finds work as a messenger boy for the advertising department of a newspaper, (Mannin, 1925 p9). He rejects his class as simple fools, despises most people and women in particular, for he sees them as responsible for men's weakness and vulnerability.

'Sounding Brass' is a satirical attack on men's attitude to women at that time. Rickard sees his first youthful attraction to Lavinia as a threat to his career prospects.

"Women were a spare-time amusement. But work, money, power, the whole getting on game, that was a man's life. That was vital. You could do without women - you were, in fact, better to do without them, for they consumed your energy, your time, and your money, all vital things - but you could not do without money" (Mannin, 1925 p86).

Despite a doting secretary Rickard marries for money but infatuation for a calculating young woman leads to his downfall. He finds that his mistress has been using him to get a divorce and that his wife only married him in the hope of getting a title. However, his fall from grace in business and society does not disturb him - he negotiates to sell his story, "The Press...that's power", and go on lecture tours of America propounding the

Ethics of Love for "I must have money....You can't get anywhere without money" (ibid, p316). In this novel Mannin clearly shows how society, ruled by patriarchal capitalism, places money above women in order of importance.

Like Mannin, Catherine Cookson sees men and women as victims of their desires. A common theme of working-class novels is the characters' desire to get on in the world. In men this is expressed as a desire for money and power but in women it is expressed as a desire for fulfilment in personal relationships, or personal achievement. Cookson started writing one book a year from 1950 and from her host of novels I have chosen 'The Round Tower' by virtue of the fact that it was awarded a literary prize, The Winifred Holtby Award[3], for the best regional novel of 1968. Some critics of popular romantic fiction blame a "capitalist 'culture industry' for the destruction of working-class consciousness and the 'massification' of culture", (Batsleer et al. 1985 p87), and because her novels often follow the formula of romantic fiction Cookson's work is usually dismissed as popularist. This does not do justice to the detailed accounts she gives of working-class lives in the North of England from the nineteenth century to the present day.

The plot of 'The Round Tower' is essentially that of class struggle. The domestic servant's son, Angus, marries the boss's daughter, Vanessa, by default (she is pregnant by another man). She grows to love Angus and his common ways as he strives to reach the same power and status as her father and eventually make good. Angus is a foreman in a factory but dismissal means that he starts his own business as a haulage contractor and thereby makes his fortune. The story is set in a Northern town in the early 1960s where the local dignitaries' humble origins are hidden. Cookson's novels are blamed for using heredity to replace and displace class struggle as the motor of history which may act "as a systematic misrepresentation of the basic conflicts of modern capitalist societies", (Batsleer et al. 1985 pp87-8). However, it could be argued that at least she acknowledges class consciousness and is not frightened to set her stories within the reality of economic necessities, something which popular romances are reluctant, if not positively averse, to doing.

Some critics are scathing of overtly political literature. To them literariness is inherent in style and form and only to found in myth and imagination or poetry. Storm Jameson claimed that "Kate Roberts is too fine a writer to arrest her explorations and her sensitivity at the shallow level of direct political statement" (Roberts, 1946, p.13) and yet acknowledges that Robert's stories reveal energy and vigour in poverty and concedes that "her work grows out of necessity; it is an art of the almost bare rocks. This is its greatest virtue" (ibid). It would seem that working-class women writers are sufficiently gifted in crafting a story so that the conditions in which they write blend into the text without overtly hammering home the political statements that they engender.

Feminism, Women and the Matriarch

"We are what we are by what we have experienced." (Mannin, 1930, p.9)

Until the second World War feminism had been primarily a middle-class interest. Only the relatively affluent had time to disect their lives and find them lacking in purpose. Bourgeois capitalism led to a social group of women who became confined to the house, in a mildly supervisory capacity, with the responsibility for housework and child-rearing placed on domestic servants. Technology began to replace domestic labour but middle-class wives still found their major role was as companions to the male head of the household and were effectively de-masculinated, having no role outside the home. Virginia Woolf, was especially concerned with liberating these women, giving them the space and income to write if they wished and the opportunity to compete with men in academic and intellectual circles. However she was singularly unconcerned with the world around her and could not relate to the millions of women socially beneath her. For these working-class women, the home and family often provided their only means of expression. The cleanliness of the home and the behaviour of the family was the only yardstick by which they could measure their success and define their status. "In short, one look at Meri Ifan's home was enough to convince that housework was akin to poetry and not a wearying and a drudgery." (Roberts, 1946, p.93).

Woolf believed that the only way to provide women with opportunity was to give them a room of their own and sufficient income to enable these 'daughters of educated men' to find their place in the literary world. The daughters of working-class men meanwhile struggled against all odds merely to write and could not afford the indulgence of a female aesthetic. Jessie Kesson admired Woolf but her background could not have been more different. Illegitimate and born in a workhouse, Kesson's life provides material for her novel 'The White Bird Passes', (1959), and "the style which emerges is elegant, confident, and unencumbered, the perfect vehicle for expressing the naivety and complexity of the developing consciousness of a young girl. It is a style which sees clearly, records accurately, and overstates nothing" (Todd, 1989 p388). The story, set in Scotland in the 1920's, recounts the childhood years of Janie who lives with her mother, Liza, in Lady's Lane; an alley rather than a road, the home of prostitutes under the guardianship of the 'Duchess' and her henchwomen, Poll and Battleaxe, who see that protocol (such as who uses which of the two toilets in the Lane) is observed.

Life for Janie is spent running errands for the women in order to earn a few pence to relieve her poverty. She and her mother live in fear of the cursory invasions of the 'Cruelty Inspector', the 'Sanitary Man' or the 'School Board Man' but still "The Lane was home and wonderful" (Kesson, 1980 p86). Janie loves her mother and is fearful that she may get involved and injured in one of the street brawls that the women of the street are prone to. Liza is undemonstrative and yet, with her gift for story telling and knowledge of local history, imbues Janie with a love of poetry and scholarly ambition. However, before she is nine years old the 'Cruelty Man' comes, Liza and Janie have to go to court and the 'Vigilance Officer' takes Janie, head now shaven, to an orphanage one hundred miles away. Janie sees her mother only once again when Liza, sick and staggering, nearly blind, visits the orphanage before she dies of syphilis. Recollecting her mother's tales Janie says "And I myself would be blind now, if she had never lent me her eyes" (Kesson, 1980 p129). The story ends, when Janie is sixteen years old, with the trustees of the orphanage deciding her future before she leaves. A trustee suggests that she takes an under-housemaid's job and someone else suggests farmwork but "Janie found the small Trustee's face. 'I don't want to dust and polish,' she told it. 'And I don't want to work on a farm. I want to write poetry. Great Poetry. As great as Shakespeare.'" (ibid p150).

Written with the unselfconscious realism typical of working-class women writers, Kesson's novel is essentially about a woman's world in which men have only walk-on parts and those in authority are titled impersonally. It certainly meets the criteria of a feminist novel, foregrounding women and their lack of opportunity, and is worthy of note.

Although Ethel Mannin occasionally made men the central characters of her novels, all the women writers in this study foreground the lives and experiences of women. Both Penn and Thompson recall periods of close friendship with girls close to their own age which are recognised as important formative relationships in a young girls life. Mannin's novel 'Linda Shawn' follows the growth of Linda from childhood and through adolescence until her fifteenth birthday. Her account of the character's development is non-judgemental and sympathetic. The natural progression of Linda's love for her father, her brother, Rose (her mother's helper), and God lead on to her love of Garry, a fisherman who dies at sea. As she copes with her grief, Linda sees herself as bound up with the cycle of the moon and caught up in its 'life-rhythm' as she crosses the threshold from child to adult.

Woolf and other modernist writers inspired an individualism that became solipsistic and feminist criticism admires this trait for concentrating on women's centrality. Working-class women writers have retained women's centrality without the exclusivity of the female aesthetic used by the modernists - namely, the stream-of-consciousness technique. Indeed, Ethel Carnie was much more generous and embraced women's specificity, their female qualities, as part of a sisterhood which stood united against the tyranny of an economic (and patriarchal) oppression, which should be equally gratifying to the feminist critic.

"When Carrie began to feel less awkward at the tasks Fanny set her, and had a little time to look round, she felt that she loved the girls. Poverty has no deceit, and they got to know each other quickly. Some thirty girls and women worked in the long, whitewashed rooms, and when they were really serious, singing some old hymn tune, or a popular ditty of the day, there was a sense of brave, beautiful fellowship about them, transforming them from so many cranks in a mighty machine into living souls."

(Carnie, 1913, p.159)

It should be of interest to the feminist critic to observe the portrayal of all the women in these works. Not only are the lives of women foregrounded but frequently women are shown as strong and determined and a matriarchal figure within society is often presented. In a working-class environment she is vital to the social and economic survival of her family and the community. These women do not rail at their position as manager of the household affairs. Their struggle against poverty is as acute as their husbands. However, many are frustrated by their husband's lack of drive and ambition or income. Some, like Hilda Winstanley's mother, Lizzie, in Penn's 'Fourteen Miles to Manchester', press their husbands to leave the relative security of their employment and take up new jobs. Forsaking his work as a farm labourer and becoming a road ganger, Joe Winstanley is not only guaranteed regular hours and 21s a week but, by working for the council, he achieves improved social status. His reluctance to make the change is treated by Lizzie scathingly,

> "Reckon you're a barm-pot then, Joe Winstanley. Us 'as got to look out for oursen and 'tisn't every chap as gets t'chance o' working for t'Council, as tha knows very well. Ah've no patience wi' your gormless ways." (Penn, 1979, p.132).

The 3s per week extra in his wages meant that Lizzie demanded a bigger house. In her new rented house she could now have a 'proper' front room and her growing daughters could sleep in a separate bedroom from their older brothers and not have to share a room divided by a curtain.

Mannin shows in 'Linda Shawn' that the frustration of Linda's mother, Ellen, is especially keen for, as a school teacher, her marriage to a third generation Irish tenant farmer is considered beneath her. Andrew Shawn proves to be unambitious and contented, living day to day unaffected by others' opinions. Ellen becomes disappointed and embittered and, the antithesis of Andrew, resorts to nagging and complaining. Her only hope for improvement lies in her children, that they should do well at school, go on to matriculate and then on to college. Despite her marriage, Ellen's personal status remains and when the local vicar wished to re-introduce the festival of 'Apple-Christening' he went "to discuss the matter with Ellen Shawn; as an educated woman, he pointed out, she would appreciate the value of preserving those traditions in rural life which the rush and cynicism of modern life threatened to exterminate" (Mannin, 1947, p.170). Mannin succeeds in conveying contemporary attitudes and values which, on the face of it, collude with sexual ideology whilst at the same time cast doubt on their validity. These are reflected in Ellen's indifference to her daughter about whose growth and development she observes, "it was no joke growing to be a woman. A man wouldn't understand that. Men didn't understand these things. Men were different." (Mannin, 1947, p.83). And of Linda's education she thinks "It would not matter so much if she failed to pass examinations; there would always remain for her the possibility of a good marriage; a career wasn't so important for a girl", (ibid, p.63). But she concedes "outside of a good marriage, what was there for the child? Nothing but drudgery, Ellen thought, drudgery and disappointment." (ibid)

In Cookson's 'The Round Tower', the only novel of this study to be set in the period after the Second World War, the influence of women over their menfolk, intentionally or otherwise, is an important strand to her story. The central male figure, Angus, achieves his position in the factory due to his mother's position in the manager's household. The manager's wife is anxious to retain her valued domestic help. Angus' mother, Emily, a widow, is the matriarchal figure who has kept the family together and been willing to suffer bad treatment to see her son get on. He, in turn, is devoted to his mother and vows to look after her in the future. But it is Angus' idolising love for the manager's daughter that contributes to his ambition to succeed as a businessman and Cookson successfully weaves working-class attitudes into a story of awakening love in which romance plays little part.

It may be argued that such presentations of women in literature simply reinforce the capitalist ideology of the importance of man as the dominant wage-earner and hence the head or master of the household. Women before the Second World War, it is true, were kept in such a position of financial dependence that today they are regarded as having been socially and sexually oppressed. What working-class literature succeeds in portraying, however, is that despite such oppression women were seen as a force to be reckoned with. I would suggest that male dominance is largely a product of affluence and middle-class ideology; that a woman as an individual is lost when poverty has been overcome, when the joint struggle for survival develops into a more sharply defined sexual division of labour and eventually into competition for financial status and security. Mannin's 'Sounding Brass' reflects this and an underlying theme of the story is the position of women in society. It illustrates a fear of the power of women; Rickard fights sexual desire and recognises birth control as an instrument of power. He sees that the First World War has helped to emancipate women, "But the country was still run by a masculine government and the Press was owned and organised by men, and men it was who conducted the country's trade, and made roads and organised railways and built palaces of commerce. Woman was still, in vital matters, a negligible quantity"

(Mannin, 1925 p90). Giving the character of Rickard the reassurance he needs to confirm his superiority, Mannin skillfully illustrates the plight of women in the 'established order', (ibid) and sees the irony of their so-called emancipation.

At this time women's emancipation was still largely the concern of the middle class yet, in working-class women's literature, women's character and individualism could still be expressed. That such women were able to assert themselves within the family and society under the prevailing conditions is only to be admired. Indeed, 'Women's Liberation' was seen to be budding in the 1880s. In Thompson's Lark Rise only three of the thirty cottages had their own water supply and it was necessary for the women to make the regular journey to the well.

> "A few of the younger, more recently married women who had been in good service and had not yet given up the attempt to hold themselves a little aloof would get their husbands to fill the big red store crock with water at night. But this was said by others to be 'a sin and a shame', for after his hard day's work, a man wanted his rest, not to do 'oman's work'. Later on in the decade it became the fashion for the men to fetch water at night and then, of course, it was quite right that they should do so and a woman who 'dragged her guts out' fetching more than an occasional load from the well was looked upon as a traitor to her sex." (Thompson, 1973, p22)

However, despite the awareness of some that domestic duties should be shared, the physical power and mental weakness of some men could be misplaced and the mistreatment of women by their husbands is not overlooked. There were a small number who were victims of their passive natures and their violent or drunken husbands, but many fought back. Queenie of Lark Rise, when beaten by her drunken husband who was suitably ashamed afterwards, brought the point home by serving him a pie in which she had baked his belt. "But it cured 'en, for's not so much as laid a finger on me from that day to this", (ibid, p86). More extreme measures were taken by Hilda Winstanley's natural grandmother, Grandma Stringer, when her daughter was the regular victim of a violent husband. Whilst he was in a drunken stupour she enlisted the aid of other men in the family to lift him onto a sheet. She proceeded to sew him tightly into it so that he could not move and then set about him, thrashing him with his own belt until he screamed for mercy. Ordering the others not to interfere,

> "Mrs Stringer was demoniac. Again and again and yet again she brought down the strap...'That'll larn thee, Jonah Turton, to treat my girl like a dog. And her childer. And if tha lays a hand on her again, or on t'childer, Ah'll not answer for what happens to thee" (Penn, 1979, p.51)

As these stories illustrate, many women had a strength of character that would not allow them to be passive. They may not have had any financial refuge from their partners but their feelings could be expressed in strong and forthright ways. The fact that, in general, both sexes considered women's role as matriarch and household manager to be of importance and influence in a society largely unresponsive to the inequalities of sex and class, was an achievement in itself. Similarly these women authors had the strength and determination to write about such experiences against the odds. It was not only lack of income and patriarchal oppression that restricted their success and reknown but, despite their contemporary popularity amongst the 'masses', an historical process that has traditionally denied women and the working classes from having a voice.

Conclusion

> "Belief in a chosen few writers as part of an intellectual and spiritual elite in a world of mass shoddiness is less popular now than it was; it can still be found but its heyday was in the years between the wars and for some little time thereafter." (Hewitt, 1988, p.172)

So why have these working-class women writers failed to be considered by literary critics, and feminist critics in particular? Carnie and Mannin were popular authors of their time as is Cookson today. How else could Cookson and Mannin have sustained such a prolific flow of publications? One must therefore assume that they were not considered worthy of critical acclaim. Considered worthy by whom? This final chapter seeks to explain the position of these writers within the literary hierarchy of the twentieth century

The study of English literature is a relatively new phenomenon within academia. Until the late nineteenth century a thorough knowledge of the classics, Greek and Latin, epitomised the educated or intellectual man. The prevention of a secular intelligentsia by the aristocracy in earlier centuries had led to the linking of intellectuals with the ruling classes. The social structure that evolved with the development of the Industrial Revolution led to a new middle class and a huge underclass. Ignorant and underprivileged, these masses were seen to pose a threat to the stability of society. Nineteenth century scholars and philosophers, such as Matthew Arnold, felt that education would smooth away the rough edges of these philistines and teach them the acceptable values and morals of their 'betters'. Arnold believed that literature could provide a social enlightenment to its readers that would ensure their co-operation in preserving the status quo.

English criticism, therefore, became a tool to ensure that such enlightenment was enforced, and pursued what Chris Baldick describes as a social mission. He identifies three principle factors which placed the study of literature high on the agenda of educationalists of the nineteenth century - the needs of the British Empire with regard to admission to the India Civil Service, the move towards adult education in Mechanics Institutes and Working Men's Colleges, and the demand for specific provision for women's education (Baldick, 1983, p.61). These factors were to mould the way in which English was taught. It was considered an important subject to be learnt alongside the profusion of technical subjects that industrial growth demanded in order "to promote sympathy and fellow feeling among all classes," (Anon, cited Baldick, 1983. p.62). Whilst the intention was to detract from any revolutionary ideas the working class may have harboured its result was to foster a need for improvement and self cultivation among them as posed by literature. Literature began to embody a 'political culture' which created certain standards, a need for a common respect for national values, a solidarity and patriotism, that led to a class inferiority. This made working-class readers less confident about their own abilities to write or communicate, in effect "numbing their own creative capacity", (ibid, p.67).

The idea of culture as an intellectual, spiritual and material way of life developed with the Industrial Revolution and human skills became categorised and distinguishable from one another. "Artist had meant a skilled person, as had artisan; but artist now referred to those selected skills [imaginative, creative] alone," (Williams, 1971, p.15). The status of the artist - the painter, musician or writer - was changing and by the early nineteenth century the growth of the middle-class reading public had led to the growth of a literary market. The successful writer became a 'professional man' with new independent status. An ideology developed in which a distinction was made between mental and manual labour and this served to oppress the working classes even further, whilst making it acceptable for the male professional writer to work in the recently evolved 'feminine' sphere of home rather than in the public domain of men.

Meanwhile the exlusion of women from scientific and classical studies in higher education resulted in them studying English Literature in greater numbers. Unfortunately this was not designed to offer them greater opportunity but to reinforce the ideology that middle-class women would be able to exercise a moderating and humanising effect on their husbands. "A vast cultural production relegating women to houshold management while 'authors' wrote made it difficult for middle-class women to write" (Gagnier, 1989, p.39).

The failure of academia to embrace the new industrial society had created an alienation which led to the professionalisation of universities and the development of an aesthetic movement. Writers and thinkers, not wishing to be linked with the production of popular literature, strived to be isolated from the market place and the general public, and in doing so wished to rise above the middle classes and create an atmosphere of high culture. The search for greater knowledge led to specialisation and hence to the creation of a select group of male Literary Critics.

Those middle-class women who did succeed in writing for publication, not surprisingly, found themselves caught up in a double standard. To be considered worthy of readership they had to uphold ideals of femininity and delicacy of expression, for only men were seen capable of writing 'universal truths' and only men were thought able to have access to the full range of human experience, (Burlinson in Buck, 1992, p.23). The 'new woman' at the turn of the century, intent on confirming women's role as the 'spiritual guardian of the race', did little to undermine this ideology, (ibid, p.26).

For the working classes of this period, publication and critical reception of their work had to overcome other social perceptions. The desire of working-class men to write was seen as potentially seditious, linked with political crisis and social unrest. As a nineteenth-century writer, Charles Fleming, noted in his article 'The Difficulties of Appearing in Print' it was necessary to establish "a line of distinction between the class who are to write and the class who are to read" and that "a single glance at the pages of a working man will cause them to be pronounced 'too vulgar for publication'" (Maidment, 1987, p.332). However, the awakening of a social conscience did open the way to stories about the working class, made acceptable with stories by Dickens and Gaskell, but these were directed at the middle class. By the turn of the century the increased literacy of the lower classes had led to a mass readership which demanded a market, of what is frequently referred to as inferior material, of its own. This was to unsettle the established literary writers "who knew almost nothing and felt little commonality of interests and values" with working-class readers" (Heyck, 1982, p.199).

Raymond Williams sees this period as generating a new mass culture out of the mob "and the traditional characteristics of the mob were retained in its significance: gullibility, fickleness, herd-prejudice, lowness of taste and habit. The masses, on this evidence, formed the perpetual threat to culture" (Williams, 1971, p.288). The fear of anarchy which had led to social control through education and the imposition of a stamp tax on books to make them too expensive for a working-class readership who may have developed ideas above their station, had given way to an awareness that popular culture could be produced for the working classes by others for political or commercial reasons. Newspapers were founded which were aimed at the working classes but the mass readership of literature became synonymous with women's fiction. Novelettes and halfpenny romances dominated the market and "such success contributed to the picture of a reading public divided between a cultured masculine elite and a mass readership predominantly female and catered for by females" (Trodd, 1991, p.10).

There was a tendency to characterise Victorian literature as innately feminine. Middle-class women had begun to write openly, rather than use male pseudonyms, for they could now meet the needs of the growing market for popular fiction. The idea of writing as a feminine activity lingered on amongst the working classes until the second World War, "I never thought of becoming a professional writer. In the first place it was somehow feminine...a man found his place through his muscular strength and ability, or agility...These were masculine things and writing was very effeminate", states Sid Chaplin, a miner-cum-writer, (Hawthorn, 1984, p.143). Working-class men overcame this disadvantage by disguising their literature under the veil of socialism, by using realism to engage with a didactic political message. Tressel's novel, for example, was designed to exclude the middle class and enlighten and inform the working classes about socialism. Few working-class women, however, had the opportunity to rise above the demands of domestic life. "It would have been quite impossible for any of the poor, struggling, coping women...to have won the time or quiet to put pen to paper;" (Beauman, 1983, p100).

Middle-class men resorted to elitism and institutionalisation to preserve their male superiority in the literary domain. The early twentieth century saw a move to establish an English tradition of literature with the 'Establishment Literati', such as Conrad, Hardy, James and Yeats, founding an academic committee in 1910. F.R.Leavis was later to place literary criticism at the same level of importance. His creation of a canon of literature was symbolic of the selectivity and hierarchy that was to develop in the professionalisation of English literature. Standards were set and criteria to be met that narrowed the perceptions and appreciation of literature and were enshrined in syllabuses which excluded minor writers. James is quoted as calling the novel "so preponderantly cultivated among us by women, in other words by a sex ever gracefully, comfortably, enviably unconscious...of the requirements of form" (Trodd, 1991, p.6)

The range of authors, from a variety of backgrounds, who succeeded at the turn of the century had, by the 1930s, been replaced by a narrow group of approved writers from the same social background. Namely, male public schools and redbrick universities which bred "such self-confident literary castes as the members of the Bloomsbury Group and the dominant literary editors and reviewers of the inter-war years" (Hewitt, 1988, p.199).

Thus, by implication, arose the idea that what is read by the masses or written by the relatively unknown is not good literature or worthy of criticism. Women, obviously, fell into this category and some influential women in the past compounded this view. The dominance of romantic fiction in mass readership was embarrassing to feminists and was seen as the result of the lack of a significant role for women in society. Olive Schreiner writes in her polemic 'Women and Labour' 1911,

> "Even in the little third-rate novelist whose works cumber the ground, we see often a pathetic figure, when we realise that beneath that failure in a complex and difficult art, may lie buried a sound legislator, an able architect, an original scientific investigator, or a good judge...Both the creative writer and the typist, in their respective spheres, are merely finding outlets for their powers in the direction of least resistance." (cited Trodd, 1991, p.71).

Women such as Schreiner, resenting their lack of opportunity to compete with men in a patriarchal world were blind to the fact that the same men were creating standards and criteria in order to exclude women and the majority of other men from competing. The 'third-rate novelist', who may have been doing what she wanted or, at least, what a reading public demanded, was labelled as the result of perceptions of taste that had been trained by a male dominated society. But, more importantly, the working classes wanted to read about themselves, to see themselves and their lives reflected in literature. Recognition of their lives would mean that their suffering and toil was worth something. As it was, their stories had been lost through the selectivity of established literary and publishing circles; their existence and experience had not been worthy of a place in literature or history.

The insidious degrading and downgrading of mass culture is reiterated by another woman who lived with an equally eminent and influential husband. Q.D.Leavis wrote:-

> "The training of the reader who spends his leisure in cinemas, looking through magazines and newspapers, listening to jazz music, does not merely fail to help him, it prevents him from normal development...partly by providing him with a set of habits inimical to mental effort. Even in small matters it gets in his way: for example, the preconceptions acquired from the magazine story and the circulating library novel are opposed to any possibility of grasping a serious novelist's intention."

(Baldick, 1983, p.217)

Such powerful figures, although often well meaning in their defence of a self-defined literary standard, not only cut the ground out from under the feet of the masses but created barriers that middle-class women struggled to breach. They succeeded in reinforcing the ideology that women were only fit to write populist novels and therefore, by implication, were not serious enough to be worthy of a critical reading. In order to compete with successful men writers, women such as Dorothy Richardson and Virginia Woolf had sufficient social standing to be able to create a new style of writing and persuade certain literary circles of its exclusivity. A movement developed which felt the need to break with convention and create a new aestheticism. "One of the unconscious motives behind the view that artists must break with convention was surely a sense of belonging to a socially defined minority of superior souls", (Hewitt, 1988, p.134). Just as working-class writers were finding their feet and competently producing acceptable realist novels, modernism was introduced that effectively undermined them. Only the privileged could afford to indulge in this new style, a style which saw people not as social creatures but as individuals in an alien society. The stream-of-consciousnesss technique embodied in the work of modernist writers was seen as a distinctly feminine method of writing.

This came at a time when Britain was entering a severe economic depression. The mass unemployment of these years provided working-class men with enforced leisure time and thus the motivation and opportunity to write. The period had an adverse effect on the lives of women. Rarely classified as unemployed, the tedium of domestic life was never lightened and in fact became harder at this time when all their energy was spent skimping and scraping and devising ways to make ends meet. With the exception of Ethel Mannin, who was by this time a popular author, I have not found evidence of any working-class woman writer coming to the fore in the 1930s. Yet, by the end of this period readers were demanding novels with their own backgrounds, "...radical working-class writers of fifty years ago were welcomed by the reading public. They took the novel to places where it had never been before - down a pit, on a dole queue, in a working-class kitchen" (Croft, 1990, p.17). It seems that there were only male authors able to meet this demand, for literary output by women came predominantly from the middle classes and so working-class women had to be content with representations of other lives. However, as Andy Croft goes on to say of one of the rare examples of a woman working-class writer, "The popular romantic fiction of a writer like Ethel Mannin, for example, may tell us more about the hopes and fears of more people in Britain in the 1930s than endlessly reading Virginia Woolf will." (ibid).

In all probability British working-class women in the first half of the twentieth century just did not have the strength or confidence to write novels, or literature generally, and, if they did, I feel sure it was hidden away and has been forgotten. At any rate, I can find only the afore-mentioned women and I am disappointed that feminist critics have not commented on the fact of such women's omission from women's literary history. The desire of early twentieth century feminist writers to achieve status in the predominantly male literary world, the creation of stream-of-consciousness style of writing and the rejection of the authorial 'I' as a masculine trait, although of worthy intention, effectively hindered the development and recognition of working-class women. This came at a time when, through education and on ground established by their male counterparts, they may just have been gaining confidence. I leave it to Tony Davies, (Hawthorn, 1984, p136), to have the final word:-

"...the Women's Movement has offered a reminder in recent years, that a collective consciousness, if it is to be active and useful, has to be built and defended: recovered from the past, redefined and consolidated in the present."

Notes

1. See main list for a short resume of these writers' lives.
2. Robert Tressel wrote 'The Ragged Trousered Philanthropists' which achieved only a mass 'underground' readership until its publication after his death, in an abridged form, in 1914. It was not published unabridged until 1955.
3. Winifred Holtby, 1898-1935, was a journalist, novelist, dramatist and social reformer. With her close friend, Vera Brittain, she actively campaigned for pacificism and women's rights, (Buck, 1992, p641).

BIBLIOGRAPHY

Primary Sources

CARNIE, Ethel. (1913) Miss Nobody, Methuen & Co. Ltd.

COOKSON, Catherine. (1992) The Round Tower, Warner Books.

KESSON, Jessie. (1959) The White Bird Passes, Chatto and Windus.

KESSON, Jessie. (1963) Glitter of Mica, Hogarth Press.

KESSON, Jessie. (1985) Where the Apple Ripens, Chatto and Windus.

MANNIN, Ethel. (1925) Sounding Brass, London, Jarrolds.

MANNIN, Ethel. (1930) Impressions and Confessions, London, Jarrolds.

MANNIN, Ethel. (1947) Linda Shawn, London, Jarrolds Ltd.

PENN, Margaret. (1979) Manchester Fourteen Miles, Caliban Books.

ROBERTS, Kate. (1946) A Summer Day, Cardiff, Penmark Press Ltd.

THOMPSON, Flora. (1973) Lark Rise to Candleford, Penguin Books.

WILKINSON, Ellen. (1989) Clash, Virago Press.

Secondary Sources

ASHRAF, P. M., (1979) Introduction to Working Class Literature in Great Britain, Lehrmaterial zur Ausbildung von Diplomlehren Englisch.

BALDICK, Chris. (1983) The Social Mission of English Criticism, 1848-1932. Oxford, Clarendon Press.

BATSLEER, J., DAVIES, T., O' ROURKE, R. WEEDON, C. (1985) Rewriting English: Cultural politics of gender and class. Methuen & Co.

BEAUMAN, Nicola. (1993) A Very Great Profession - The Woman's Novel 1914 - 39, Virago Non-Fiction.

BLAIN, CLEMENTS & GRUNDY, (1990) The Feminist Companion to English Literature. London, B.T.Batsford, Ltd.

BRADBURY, Malcolm, (1971) The Social Context of Modern English Literature, Basil Blackwell.

BUCK, Claire, (ed), (1992) Bloomsbury Guide to Women's Literature, Bloomsbury Publishing

BURNETT, J., VINCENT, D. & MAYALL, D. (1984,87) The autobiography of the working class: an annotated critical bibliography, Volumes 1 and 2, The Harvester Press.

DYHOUSE, Carol. (1981) Girls Growing Up in Late Victorian and Edwardian England, Routledge & Keegan Paul Ltd.

EAGLETON, Mary, & PIERCE, David. (1979) Attitudes to Class in the English Novel, Thames & Hudson.

EAGLETON, Mary. (ed) (1991) Feminist Literary Criticism, Longman.

FOSTER, John. (1974) Class Struggle and the Industrial Revolution, Weidenfeld & Nicholson.

FREEMAN, Charles. (1985) Britain in the 1930s, Batsford Academic & Educational.

HAWTHORN, Jeremy. (1984) The British Working-Class Novel in the Twentieth Century, Edward Arnold.

HEWITT, D. (1988) English Fiction of the Early Modern Period 1890-1940, Longman Group.

HEYCK, T.W. (1982) The Transformation of Intellectual Life in Victorian England, Croom Helm.

HICKEN, Mandy, & PRYTHERCH, Ray. (1990) Now Read On...A guide to contemporary popular fiction, Gower.

KEATING, P.J. (1971) The Working Classes in Victorian Fiction, Routledge & Keegan Paul.

KLAUS, H. Gustav. (1985) The Literature of Labour: 200 Years of Working-Class Writing, The Harvester Press.

KLAUS, H. Gustav. (1987) The Rise of Socialist Fiction 1880-1914, The Harvester Press.

MAIDMENT, Brian. (1987) The Poorhouse Fugitive, Carcanet Press

NIELD CHEW, Doris. (1982) Ada Nield Chew: The Life and Writings of a Working Woman, Virago.

ROBERTS, Elizabeth. (1984) An Oral History of Working-Class Women 1890-1940, Basil Blackwell

SCHLUETER, Paul & June (eds). (1988) An Encyclopedia of British Women Writers, Garland Publishing Inc.

SMITH, David. (1978) Socialist Propoganda in the Twentieth-Century British Novel, MacMillan.

SWINDELLS, Julia. (1985) Victorian Writing and Working Women, Polity Press.

THOLFSEN, Trygve R. (1976) Working-Class Radicalism in Mid-Victorian England, Croom Helm.

TRODD, Anthea. (1991) A Reader's Guide to Edwardian Literature, Harvester Wheatsheaf.

TODD, Janet. (1989) Dictionary of British Women Writers, Routledge.

WILLIAMS, Raymond. (1971) Culture and Society 1780-1950, Penguin.

Chapters

FROW, Edmund & Ruth. (1985) 'Ethel Carnie: writer, feminist and socialist', in KLAUS, H. Gustav. The Rise of Socialist Fiction, 1880-1914, The Harvester Press.

LODGE, David. (1969) 'The Novelist at the Crosswords', in BRADBURY, Malcolm (ed). (1977) The Novel Today Manchester University Press, Rowan & Littlefield/Fontana Books.

WEBSTER, Wendy. (1992) 'Our Life: Working-Class Women's Autobiography in Britain', in BONNER, F. GOODMAN, L. et al. (eds), Imagining Women - Cultural Representations and Gender, Polity Press.

Articles

COOKSON, Catherine. (1987) 'My First Book'. The Author, Spring, pages 7-9.

CROFT, Andy. (1990) 'Left on the Shelf'. The Listener, October, pages 16-17.

DUCHENE, Anne. (1981) 'Home Comforts'. Times Literary Supplement, July 24, page 830.

DUSINBERRE, Juliet. (1984) 'The Child's Eye and The Adult's Voice: Flora Thompson's Lark Rise to Candleford.' Review of English Studies, Number 35, Feb 84, pages 61-70.

GAGNIER, Regenia. (1989) 'The Literary Standard, Working-class lifewriting and gender. Textual Practice Volume 3, Number 1, Spring, 1989 pages 36-55.

MANNIN, Ethel. (1974) '50 years this week with the same publisher'. The Bookseller, 7 Dec, pages 2842-4.

O'ROURKE, Rebecca. (1988) 'Were There No Women? British Working-Class Writing in the Inter-War Period'. Literature and History, Volume 14:1, Spring, pages 48-63.

Writing and the Miners' Strike 1984-5

by Sammy Palfrey

Introduction

This paper was originally given as part of a History Workshop weekend event at Ruskin College in 1992, 'Hidden Histories'. It forms part of a research project *'Working-class Writing - Three Recent Models'* [1] , the Miners' Strike being the most recent example at that time of spontaneous writing brought about through struggle and political upheaval, and therefore offering a different model of writing practice to the other two areas of working-class writing that were looked at.

As I had to restrict my research, given the enormous volume of writing and publications that came out of the strike, I limited myself geographically by concentrating the research in Yorkshire, where the strike started and where the media and police concentrated a lot of their activities. Whilst staying with Jean Miller, founding member of the Barnsley Women Against Pit Closures (which was where the Women Against Pit Closures movement got off the ground, and where the group managed to produce two publications during the year of the strike) I was able to meet many of the women from that group and from other mining villages in Yorkshire who wrote during the strike and who helped produce the books.

Many people view the 1984 Miners' Strike as a failure, especially when in 1995 even more coal mines have been closed than Arthur Scargill predicted. But interviewing women from the mining community in Yorkshire revealed that for many of them the Strike is seen as one of the most important and fulfilling years of their lives. The writing was an integral part of the year-long struggle; it provided a means of fund-raising for the strike and of being a written endorsement of the solidarity experienced during that year.

It has provided a lasting documentation and testimony to that struggle from the people involved, and can stand firmly beside the work of historians and journalists. But it is not just the products that should be studied when looking at this body of writing; the way that the production of literature was organised and processed in the midst of a major political dispute is in itself a demonstration of what can be achieved through collective struggle, as too is the recognition of the intensity of local sales and attendance at poetry events by local people.

For many writers as I have shown, it was the first time that they had written anything at length like this since leaving school; if they had written before they had often destroyed it, believing it to be of no value. Writing during the strike meant they received such encouragement and support from their own community, that together with the important part that the writing played in the miners' struggle, they felt a true value in their writing.

People worked collectively to produce, distribute and sell books and broadsheets. All this experience provided confidence to the writers, which has led many of them to continue writing openly, to join local writing workshops, and particularly for the women, to attend local colleges for some sort of further education or training. Writers like Madeleine Butterfield have had the opportunity to develop their writing in a local group, with new experiences that can be shared and explored at a more leisurely pace than she was able to undertake in the strike.

It could be that the Miners' Strike was the last of the great political struggles of that nature, as some political writers have claimed. That is impossible to predict, but what is certain is that the writing from the Strike, as with writing from other radical movements in the past such as the Chartist Movement, is of great value to the labour movement as it shows how far and in which ways it is possible to develop a radical class-conscious literature.

Placing the Writing: Its Value is Recognised by the Community

> "I'm fighting for you son; look back on this day,
> Your right is to work lad but also to play.
> Your mam's counting pennies and precious black coal,
> So we'll stand up and fight lad,
> your future's our goal."[2]

The Miners' Strike of 1984-5 turned out to be the longest major strike in British history, and has resulted not surprisingly in many academic works from sociological surveys to historical analysis. No less surprising in the long history of the neglect and negation of the working-class writer, there has been far less published commercially by writers from the mining communities themselves about the strike. In *The Heart And Soul Of It,* a documentation of how the strike affected the people from the pit village of Worsbrough, one of the writers noted in the introduction that

> "Whilst looking into local history for certain information about the 1926 Miners' Strike, it became apparent that too little was recorded about the people most affected by the strike".

Yet writing was an intrinsic part of the 1984-5 strike, both collectively as published documentation and poetry, broadsheets of poems sold in pubs and at fund-raising events, and privately in the form of diaries and letters. It was recognised by the striking community as an important contribution, as valuable as the other activities, because they all shared a common function; to win the strike and save the mining communities. Jean Gittins, from the North Yorkshire group of Women against Pit Closures (WAPC), who had a book of twenty poems published during the strike stated "Those that could write, wrote; those that could cook did the cooking. It was all part of the whole fight".

No-one was excluded from any activity, people fell into comfortable roles, or ventured into new ones. All activities were given equal status and validity, being seen as part of the whole fight.

Misrepresentation by the Media: A Defensive Strategy Develops

'Community under Siege' became the collective feeling of the mining communities and their supporters during the year-long strike. Their fight became not just a fight to save their whole way of life, which would be destroyed alongside the closure of the mines, but ultimately a fight against the government, the police and the media for the very right to strike. They were horrified at the behaviour of the police and disillusioned with the media, which Betty Heathfield from Sheffield WAPC stated in her introduction to *Media Hits The Pits*, raged "a remorseless campaign of prejudice, distortion and lies instigated by the Government and pushed relentlessly through the mass media".

It was this misrepresentation which was often the initial factor for leading people to write down their story of what the strike was about, and what was really going on in the striking communities; reaction was so strong that it stimulated many to write creatively for the first time since leaving school.

As Mike Coburn from Hatfield Main Colliery, Doncaster, put it

> "Not being a man of words I find it hard to do an article, but I feel nevertheless that it is something I must do. To put over my side, point of view and feelings, so others may see." (*'The Way I Saw It', in A Year In Our Lives*)

It was this defensive nature of the strike that led to the feelings of solidarity and a sense of power which in their turn created a confidence that nurtured all kinds of creative talents.

Many miners were angered by Margaret Thatcher's description of them as "The Enemy Within", a tag eagerly taken up by the media and which prompted an outraged response in the writing.

Dave Douglas, a miner from Hatfield Main Colliery, writes in the book *Tell Us Lies About The Miners*, how

> "Miners have always known that the media was biased, pro-boss, but never realised it could be used as a tool of oppression, a deliberate set-up to mould public opinion" (page 5).

This misrepresentation was the subject of poetry too; Jean Gittins in her "*Yorkshire Picket Song*" asks

> "Ah'm a picket A Yorkshire picket 'Appen some of you've seen me on TV Ah'm a picket A Yorkshire picket Do you believe exactly what you see?"[2]

Women's Support Groups: an Empowering Experience

Women were angered by the impression the media tried to give, that miners' wives were against the strike, and this led to the formation of local women's support groups, the first being Barnsley Women Against Pit Closures. Local WAPC groups then linked up to become a national organisation. It was the solidarity and democratic structure of these groups, and security from the strong sense of community they created, that gave the women self-confidence.

This confidence led many of them to discover themselves for the first time; it gave them a sense of power and belief in their own value. It was this aspect of the groups that in part empowered women to write, often for the first time, and in greater numbers than the men. Also wives and mothers found themselves with more time to be creative as in turn the men whilst on strike had more time to share with childcare and housework, when not out picketing.

So women found themselves not just with an urge to write as a response to the media and a catharsis for their anger but because they received encouragement and support from others who valued their creative abilities.

As Madeleine Butterfield, another poet whose book, *Striking Thoughts* was published at the end of the strike felt

> "The strike was an opportunity for everyone
> to discover what their talents and capabilities
> were and to put them into practice".

Madeleine, like so many working-class people, was brought up with the idea that "If working class wrote poetry they were just mimicking their betters", but found that during the strike "The impulse to write was there in your head all the time". When she wrote her first poem and took it along to her local women's' support group she pretended it was someone else's until certain that people liked it. It was through the group's encouragement that her collection was later published by the group themelves.

Miner-Poets and the *Yorkshire Miner*

Even though there were less men than women writing, many men took the opportunity of having more "above ground" time to be creative. Although there have been miner poets since the first shafts were sunk the elevated status that culture achieved during the strike made it a more acceptable activity, and miners like Bill Ross, who had previously kept his poetry a secret, was able to 'come out'. Some of his poems were featured in the 'Poets Corner' of the *Yorkshire Miner*, the Yorkshire edition of the national weekly paper of the National Union of Mineworkers (NUM), including one called *'Echoing Footsteps'*, about the sound of the ghosts of miners killed in past mining accidents and was a tribute to David Jones who was killed on the picket line during the strike.

There has always been a tradition of publishing poems in *'The Miner'*, which is published regionally. During the strike it was inundated with poems from miners and their families, So much so that despite having double-page spreads in some issues of the Yorkshire Miner the published poems still represented only a small minority of all those submitted. Many poems that were finally published in anthologies and community books of the strike were first featured in the Miner. Indeed the NUM with the help from the local WEA writing workshops' organiser put out an anthology of poems from the Miner entitled *Against All The Odds.*

This featured many poets such as Barbara Brookes whose poem *'Orgreave'*, an account of police violence at the now renowned 'Battle of Orgreave' that occurred outside the Orgreave coking plant, also demonstrates the fierce loyalty felt towards the NUM leader, Arthur Scargill, which was echoed in many other poems despite efforts by the media to discredit him.

In one of the verses she recounts

"Arthur, standing his ground Pouring strength of will and body into the gathering force, With them, of them, for them. The blue ranks parting like the Red Sea, To let the cavalry through, Hooves, truncheon and baton Against bone and flesh." (p.31)

Publication During the Strike: Its Function and Use

Publishing during the strike was not just a means of spreading the word. Its other important function, and providing just as much impetus to write, was its role as a fund-raiser and therefore its important part in helping to win the struggle. All of the pamphlets and books published provided valuable funds towards the mining community during and after the strike. Profits went either straight to the organisations that had produced them, such as local women's support groups, or most often into the Miners' Solidarity Fund, and after the return to work, into the Miner's Victimisation Fund.

Money to produce the publications came mostly from donations. These came from individual supporters but also various groups such as the London Co-operative Political Committee and local Labour Party groups. Some small publishers such as Canary Press, London, published books at cost price. Community publishers such as Yorkshire Art Circus, who along with others like Artisan and Bannerworks of Huddersfield, not only gave valuable help and advice to people publishing their own books, but also brought out their own publications on the strike.

The ease with which people were able to get their writing published during the strike was rare for any working-class writer, let alone people writing for the first time and was another boost to the confidence of would-be writers. As poet Jean Gittins said "We were definitely flavour of the month!"

Writers were given such open encouragement and status that their creative abilities blossomed, something that for many had been repressed or unrealised for most of their lives, and this influenced others into going off to try their hand at writing. Jackie Keating, a miners' wife found herself too involved in other activities to write during the strike, though she too had often written as a child but destroyed her work as she was never given that 'cultural authority' that could make her writing feel of any kind of importance.

After the strike Jackie felt a great need to write down all her experiences from that year, and she is one of the few miner's wives to have got her work published commercially, though it took until 1991. Although Jackie went on to do some editing and work for the Yorkshire Art Circus, and was looking to apply to do some studying at a local college, she was quite disillusioned at her experiences of commercial publishing and found it a disempowering experience.

The Cultural Consciousness is Raised: How It Spreads

Outside support for this writing was invaluable and the response of local organisations was quick. Northern College Barnsley (a Labour College running part-time courses that have strong links with the trade-union movement) put on extra courses during the strike including, like the local WEA, writers' workshops. Because of the dramatic change in their day to day lives for that year and the influx of outside supporters into the mining areas, who came from different backgrounds and with different experiences, many people from the communities sought wider horizons in terms of educational and creative developments. The increase in writing workshops drew not just mining people but other locals, so that the urge to be creative spilled out of the strike into the local population at large. Maurice Jones, editor of The Miner said in his foreword to *Against All The Odds*

> "Rarely, if ever, can a dispute have released upon the world such a flood of talent as the miners' strike of '84. it is as though a dam has burst, bathing and enriching the land in the waters of creativity".

One such man, who was not from the mining industry itself but lived in the locality, was Geoff Hattersley. He joined one of the workshops set up during the strike, wrote his first poem in support of the miners' cause, and is now editor of *The Wide Skirt* one of Britain's most widely distributed poetry magazines. As Ray Hearne, tutor organiser for the Yorkshire WEA told me

> "A mass of activities emerged around the strike. People's cultural consciousness' were raised. Whereas six months before the strike we were forced to abandon a poetry event at half-time that we'd held at a Miners' Welfare, one year later we performed a similar event there to a packed hall".

Evenings like this during the strike were fund-raising events for the Miners' Solidarity Fund so people were keen to support them, but Ray also realised that the kind of poetry being read during the strike (including many people reciting their own work 'from the floor') was more relevant to their present experiences; that they could now relate to poetry in a way they couldn't before. Jean Gittins found herself in quite a demand to do readings of her poetry during the strike and in her book *Striking Stuff*, wonders jokingly at the end of the strike

> "I ask you Where do I go now it's over?
> You've robbed me of my only chance of fame. I'll have to find another purpose in my life. But nothing will quite ever be the same."[4]

A Literary Education: Beginnings and Development

Not all the writers were directly involved in the writing workshops or poetry events during the strike; some joined writing groups after the strike, or took on more extensive forms of study to further their literary education, which for many began in the strike. One such person was Iris Preston, a miner's wife who decided to keep a journal not realising how long the strike would last; it grew to 25,000 words (this is still gathering dust in the library archives at Ruskin College awaiting its promised publication). After the strike she attended various writing courses and is currently studying for an English Literature degree at Sussex University. Iris had been writing since a child but had never shown it to anyone before. Her writing grew from "A need to be something, to belong somewhere. You write because it's your rainbow".

It was the confidence that came from her involvement in the activities of the strike that led her to decide on a university education.

In the opening to her journal, Iris talks about the "Round Table Conferences" that she held with her family during the strike in order to share concerns and worries, "Although to the boys it was an excuse for a bloody good nosh up". At one "conference" held at the beginning of the strike, she sums up her initial feelings of impotence and ignorance

> "Lance opened the conversation between mouthfuls of roast tater and Yorkshire pudding, putting concisely the case for striking. 'We're out and we're staying out until pit closures policy of the NCB are scrapped, and the Plan for Coal is accepted'. I didn't understand either of these two policies." (*'A Strike Diary'* in *The Enemy Within* p.101)

Writing as an Outlet for Frustrations

Unlike Iris Preston many women felt unable to share their anxieties and fears about the strike with their striking husbands, as they knew their husbands were themselves worried, and they didn't want to add to their burden. As Mel Dukes a headmistress from a school in a mining village near Grimethorpe put it

> "The miners and their wives were subject to all kinds of pressures and frustrations that remained unrecognised or unreported in national terms".

The picket line was an obvious outlet for some of these frustrations, but writing provided another kind of catharsis.

Humour: its Importance in Pit Life and During the Strike

Some of the poems written during the strike were parodies such as *'The Charge of The Mines Brigade'* which are a traditional form in mining poetry that goes back to the early nineteenth century. Parodies such as *'The Ten Commandments'* were produced alongside political pamphlets and leaflets when literacy was spreading amongst miners. Humour was present in the different forms of writing that occurred during the strike whether poetry, autobiographical accounts or diaries, and its frequent expression reflects its importance in both the struggle of mining communities during the strike and in mining life in general.

Whilst being interviewed, some of the miners and their wives recalled humorous anecdotes from the strike and explained that although writing had not been a prominent part of their culture, telling a good story, particularly a funny one, was a way that many miners eased the burden of long shifts underground. Every picket line and support group has its own humorous tale to tell, a quite common theme being the vast and unusual contingents of food sent by comrades from abroad, such as from the accounts by Rose from Featherstone about distributing food parcels, in *Strike 84-5*

> "A lot of the stuff has that Russian writing on the side. Even when you read it through the mirror it don't get any better! I just say to the lads, 'If you know what it is, pick it up'. One of the lads said 'Throw it in, our lass'll find her way round it".

Or as Iris Preston recalled the time when a lorry-load of pasta arrive from comrades in Italy,

> "There was every conceivable shape and colour and size. No-one knew what to do with it, we were falling about laughing over suggestions. Next day, doctor's surgery was packed with women - they weren't sick, but they knew his wife had been on holiday to Italy so thought she might have some recipes".

These tales are included in the poetry and prose of the books put together by various organisations and groups, enabling readers outside of the mining families to appreciate how important seeing the funny side of things is to their culture, though as Betty Wedgewood says in *'Memories of a Year'*, from *Snippets From The Strike*, not all of them were suitable for publication

> "Ee, but ar remember t'strike
> T'struggle, t'borrerin and t'like
> Laughs an' all we'ed them as well
> Some a bit too brarn to tell".

Dialect such as Betty Wedgewood uses is not common in the writing from the Miners' Strike though Jean Gittins writes in it for many of her poems. Some writers claimed it was difficult to put it down adequately on paper - it was not something they had been taught how to do at school. It occurs mostly in the humorous writing, where writers tell the need to be clearly understood was not so crucial as when writing about more serious topics.

How Inner Conflicts/Contradictions of the Strike are Revealed

Writers tried to give clear accounts of the strike, even when they had found writing a struggle and it is the least experienced that often give a perceptive and illuminating insight from an honest, if subjective, point of view. Raymond Williams describes this kind of writing as descriptive and subjective as opposed to the ideologically-charged manipulative language used by many professional writers and journalists, keen to fit their account into a particular ideology or politics.

Without the experience of using the written word to make a political point people who believed whole-heartedly in the strike nevertheless revealed some of the contradictions and ironies which occurred.

One such account came from Bob Hume in *A Year Of Our Lives*, exploding the somewhat mythical views of working-class solidarity on the picket lines. He states

> "Ninety percent (of the pickets) were fully in support of the strike, but the others were driven into the picket line by Thatcher in order to get a bit to eat, where sandwiches were being provided - single lads were driven to go picketing because they got no financial help whatsoever". (no page numbers)

Elaine Robe in *'Hatfield Main Women's Support Group'*, from the same book, shows some of the internal conflicts that existed

> "Our pit was solid, but like a lot of places there were only a minority of activists who gave everything that they had for twelve months .... There were men who could only

offer opinions, especially against women. Many women felt hurt and angry listening to complaints".

The Power of Language: A Question of Ownership

The manipulative use of language was one of the weapons that the media used against strikers. Descriptions of them as pit mobs and pit-head thugs as opposed to "heroic working miners" suggests, says Dave Douglas, in *A Year In Our Lives*, that it is the public who were being most effectively manipulated by the media, not the miners by Arthur Scargill as the media was claiming.

Pit language, the language of the mining communities, is present in the writing from the mining communities. Madeleine Butterfield in *Striking Thoughts*, refers to the habit of some wives "wearing the window out" whilst watching for their husbands to come home safely from the pit in her poem *Waiting*. It was an expression she remembered her mother using. In another poem, she uses the expression "yarning", a local term used for the way men with advanced pneumoconiosis stretch their necks to help their breathing.

The right for people to use their own language went as far as becoming a legal issue. Words such as "scab" are part and parcel of a striker's language and was first given this use in 1792, yet it was banned from the picket lines in Nottingham by the police. Several people were actually arrested for using it though as one woman recalls in *Here We Go - Women's Memories of the 1984 Strike*, a judge overturned one case, stating "This word is not abusive, it is part of the English language, and you are allowed to use it" (p.56). Frustration at this restriction led to many poems and articles about "scabs" both in the context of the strike and in the way they are seen as traitors to the working-class movement.

Making the Writing Accessible: How it Strengthened the Struggle

Chris Searle in the journal Race and Class talks about the kind of language used in the writing from the Miners' Strike in his review of Against All The Odds. He states

"Reading the poems...is like reading again the poems of the Chartists in their journals and broadsheets. There is the same mass indignation put in the simplest and most accessible forms, the same rhythms of struggle and underlying humour, the same direct and popular language immediately understood by all those taking part in the struggle and those whose solidarity and empathy goes out towards them"[5]

As Marylyn Butler states in her introduction to *Romantics, Rebels And Reactionaries*

"Poetry in a popular style might be dangerous if it became an ideological weapon in the popular cause" (p.5).

Thomas Paine who had worked in a Rotherham pit became notorious for his *Rights Of Man*, not just beause of its content but also because he sought to write in a direct language for a working-class readership.

So whilst the early aims of the defensive writing as a counter-attack against media lies may have achieved little nationally, it developed into a collective oppositional literature written in accessible language, that both strengthened the solidarity of people involved during a year long struggle, and provided a lasting account of the strike by the people themselves.

Like the Chartist movement, the striking community made no distinction between culture and politics, and in assessing the status of the writers it should be remembered that they were most often some of the main activists in the strike. But in the end as many writers remind us all those mining families who took part in the struggle should be remembered.

> "Let not their glories be forgotten when taking stock this day. So you might work tomorrow they gave blood and 12 months pay."[6]

Notes

1 *Working-Class Writing - Three Recent Models* undergraduate dissertation 1992, West London Polytechnic, Department of Humanities. Looks at three different models of writing. Firstly the Federation of Worker Writers and Community Publishers which is a national / international federation of local writing groups who meet regularly to discuss work and put out their own publications. Secondly the Miner's Strike 1984-85. Finally it looks at Yorkshire Arts Circus, the largest community publisher in Britain, particularly examining its marketing strategies and how it affects the authors' work.

2 Butterfield, Madeleine, *'Memories'* from *Striking Thoughts*, Royston Drift Branch WAPC, 1985.

3 Gittins, Jean, *"Yorkshire Picket Song"* in Yorkshire Miner, September 1984.

4 Gittins, Jean, *'What Next'* in *Striking Stuff*, p18, 1 in 12 (Publications) Collective), Bradford, 1985.

5 Searle, Chris, in Race And Class, p. 85 Vol. 26, No. 4, Spring 1985.

6 Barnsley Women Against Pit Closures, *Barnsley Women Volume 2*, back page, Barnsley Women Against Pit Closures, Yorkshire, 1985.

Bibliography

Publications of Writing from the Mining Community

Against All The Odds, National Union of Mineworkers, Sheffield, 1984.

Barnsley Women - *Women Against Pit Closures*, Barnsley Women Against Pit Closures, 1984.

Barnsley Women - *Women Against Pit Closures, Vol. 2*, Barnsley Women Against Pit Closures, 1984.

Butterfield, Madeleine, *Striking Thoughts*, Royston Drift Branch WAPC, Barnsley, 1984.

Douglass, Dave, Ed., *A Year In Our Lives*, Hooligan Press, London, 1985.

Douglass, Dave, *Tell Us Lies About The Miners - The Role Of The Media*, Dave Douglass and Others, Yorkshire, 1985.

Gittins, Jean, *Striking Stuff*, 1 in 12 (Publishing) Collective, Bradford, 1985.

Keating, Jackie *Counting the Cost -a Family in the Miners strike* Wharncliffe publishing 1991

North Women Against Pit Closures *Strike 84-5*, North Yorkshire Women Against Pit Closures, Yorkshire, 1985.

Salt, Chrys, and Layzell, Jim, *Here we Go - Women's Memories Of The 1984/5 Miners Strike*, London Political Committee, Co-operative Retail Services, London, 1985.

Soup Kitchen Authors, *Snippets Of A Strike 1984-5*, Northern College, Barnsley, 1985.

Worsbrough Community Group *The Heart And Soul Of It,* Worsbrough Community Group and Bannerworks, Yorkshire 1985.

Secondary Texts

Butler, Marylyn *Romantics, Rebels and Reactionaries* Oxford UP 1981

Callinicos, Alex, and Simons, Mike *The Great Strike*, Bookmarks, London, 1985.

Jones, David, Ed., *Media Hits The Pits*, Campaign for Press Freedom, London, 1984.

Samuel, Raphael, Bloomfield, Barbara, and Boanas, Guy, *The Enemy Within: Pit Villages and The Miners' Strike of 1984/85*, Routledge, Kegan and Paul, London, 1986.

Periodicals

Searle, Chris, Book Review: *Against All The Odds* in Race And Class Vol. 26 No. 4 Spring 1985, Institute of Race Relations, London.

Yorkshire Miner, all copies between March 1984 and February 1985

Book Publishing -
the Gentleperson's Profession?

Gail Chester

In my mid-forties I am beginning to learn how to bring
the disparate parts of my life together, and one of the
things that has helped me most is Tillie Olsen's ovular
book, *Silences* (1980). It is the volume which every
working-class woman writer should keep by her bedside
and refer to constantly. It is an extraordinary work of
research and support. It reminds us that we are not alone
and that our feelings of inadequacy are not our fault. It
invites us to contribute our own creativity to the pool of
existing material, and it certainly encouraged me to
persevere with writing this piece.

I write as a working-class Jewish woman, a published
writer, mainly of non-fiction, (political analysis, polemic,
and autobiographical reflection a speciality), and an
editor of other people's writings. I am also a lifelong
feminist who believes it is impossible to separate the
personal from the political, especially in one's writing.
The two contrasting parts of this piece fit together as
my life fits together - the intellectual and the artist, the
public and the private, the publisher and the published
(or not). Interrupted by pressing family business, I nearly
gave up on trying to pull it all together. Then I picked up
Tillie Olsen and found this:

> "The years when I should have been writing, my
> hands and being were at other (inescapable) tasks.

...The habits of a lifetime when everything else had to come before writing are not easily broken, even when circumstances now often make it possible for writing to be first; habits of years - response to others, distractibility, responsibility for daily matters - stay with you, mark you, become you. The cost of 'discontinuity' (that pattern still imposed on women) is such a weight of things unsaid, an accumulation of material so great, that everything starts up something else in me; what should take weeks takes me sometimes months to write; what should take months, takes years." (*Silences*, pages 38-39)

Most of the writers I know suffer from the discontinuities and duties that Tillie Olsen mentions. But also prominent among the activities which displace our writing is our political activism- for many of us, a task as inescapable as domestic labour or earning a living. For me, the challenge to express my own creativity is additionally complicated, because an important part of my political activity is helping other people express themselves in writing. Sometimes I do this as an editor and sometimes by helping them get published- this was how my political analysis of the publishing industry started. And then I wondered how to try and explain the inextricable link between writing and publishing and in Tillie Olsen's book I found that she had written this:

"Anthologies, text books, courses concerned with contemporary literature, tend to be made up of living writers whose names will immediately be recognised...Writers in a profit making economy are an exploitable commodity whose works are product to be marketed, and are so judged and handled...Almost all publishing houses are now owned by conglomerates who bought them for investment purposes (oh, they knew about the high costs of printing, paper, mailing, etc.) and whose only concern (necessarily) is high profit return. Why diversify, take risks, settle for modest returns, take trouble - and literature *is* trouble". (*Silences*, page 170)

But it is not only literature which is trouble. Any writing which does not immediately conform to the status quo of published material, whether in style or content, is in serious jeopardy from the people responsible for establishing the status quo - the middle- and upper-class people who fill the mainstream publishing companies.

My employment in publishing began as a political act- my desire to see radical literature of all types more widely available. Eighteen years of analysis and experience later, I am still on the outer fringes of the profession- gaining access to the heart of the middle-class dominated academic/publishing nexus has proved impossible.

Is this because of my politics, my class background, my ethnic origins or being an uppity woman? Perhaps it is the fatal combination of all four- despite having applied for a number of jobs for which I was eminently well qualified, in a variety of mainstream publishing companies, I have never been given a single interview. And it is obviously not just me who has been excluded, as a quick look round any publishing office will reveal. Clearly, there is no shortage of women employees - after all, it's poorly paid support work, so what else is new? But the women who are employed are themselves overwhelmingly middle- or upper-class, and too often, ancilliaries of the same networks which gained their fathers admittance to the club. It is unreasonable to expect the presence of large numbers of these women to radically affect the nature of what is published, not only because of their class background, but also because, in classic patriarchal fashion, women of any class background cluster disproportionately at the bottom of whichever employment hierarchy they are in, and find it hard to progress into influential management positions. Book publishing is no different.

I believe that the overwhelmingly white, middle-class domination of the industry matters greatly to the majority of us who are neither. Of course such concerns seem trivial in the face of war, famine, homelessness and disease, or pointless in the context of prophecies of the imminent demise of the book itself. But literacy is a significant issue, particularly for women, and whatever the form of transmission of information, the people controlling the media will determine the message that is conveyed. Moreover, the printed media have a lot of life yet, particularly as the motor which drives the rest of the media machine. I mean this on an ideological level, but on a practical level, it is also clear that book publishing, so long perceived as a small, cosy enclave of decency and old fashioned (i.e. middle-class paternalistic) values, has substantially become, as Olsen points out, just another element of the multi-national media industry.

This process had already started before the electronic book, but has accelerated with its arrival. Some optimists argue that the development of electronic publishing is substantially diminishing the power of the publisher as a filter between authors and readers. However, it is important to understand that while electronic publishing is particularly useful for certain types of publishing, such as reference works and the speedy transmission of the type of information traditionally found in academic papers and journals, it is reasonably clear that it is not, and is unlikely to become, a satisfactory substitute for many forms of conventional book publishing. The electronic book is already a reality into whose development conventional publishers and others are pouring millions of pounds. Do not be deluded by the hype - ordinary people will have no better access or be any better represented in the new media than they have been in the old. And while Kath Moonan presented an extremely stimulating paper at the 1994 Culture and Class conference about the participation of working-class people and women in the new technology, there is still much work to be done to overcome the male domination of the area.

The smallest summary of why I think this all matters is that by working-class people being denied access to publishing, both as publishers and authors we are being denied access to power, to the means of communicating our ideas widely. This stops us achieving sufficient access to cultural resources to develop our belief in the possibility of us effecting positive change. The mechanisms operate in all areas of publishing, but it seems useful to give two brief sketches of the sort of things that bother me.

Academic publishing is in many ways the ultimate gatekeeping activity, as you cannot get an academic job or be promoted if you are not published. It used to be that publication of articles in academic journals was sufficient to ensure employment, but these days, having published at least one book is becoming essential for promotion. And who is it that controls the publishing process? Even in journal publishing, it is often not fellow academics, who you might hope, often mistakenly, would retain some degree of intellectual integrity, but the mandarins of the publishing business, who select and reject authors and manuscripts on grounds which often bear little relation to their merit. In terms of book publishing, the main criterion seems to be the perceived size of the market, which can be related to such unacademic and subjective issues as the 'sexiness' of the author's image, the degree of controversy likely to be generated by this approach to the topic, or how fashionable the author's academic discipline is at present.

It is almost impossible to be published by an established academic publisher if you do not have a job in an academic institution, so that people who are kept out of these jobs for political or class reasons have no substantial outlet for their written work. And because publishers expect authors to have an academic job, they pay next to nothing for your writing/research, so that unless you have a private income you are prevented from doing it anyway. A recent book (*Handbook for Academic Authors*) contains five pages of advice on how to get money to subsidise the publication of your book - and it all depends on being employed in the first place.

Throughout this process, publishers retain a ruthless attachment to the idea that they are making objective assessments of the academic worth of the manuscripts they are presented with. They claim that they maintain academic standards because all manuscripts are submitted for peer review and the publisher then bases his decision to publish (or not) on the reports of these peers. What this leaves out is the prejudices and unconscious biases of the reviewer. Basically, the reviewer is the same kind of person as the publisher. Thus what is usually maintained is the status quo rather than academic standards, and what publishers justify as responding to the market adds up to controlling it. Some critical material has been written by natural scientists and information scientists about the problems of peer review as applied to articles published in journals, (for example Weeks and Kinser, 1994) but I am not aware of any similar work that has been done about book publishing.

Members of AUT (the university teachers' union) have discussed in their journal problems encountered with book publishers, but individual authors feel powerless to challenge the system which they are so dependent on for their survival. Academics in Media Studies and

Cultural Studies, who might reasonably be expected to be more aware of the operation of these processes, have been noticeable for their absence of attention to book publishing. Of course, print media in general is not very trendy these days, but I also wonder whether the critical analysis that thrives in Film Studies, for example, is because they are most unlikely ever to be invited to direct a Hollywood movie.

The myth of academic objectivity is a close relative of the myth of artistic judgement, which is usually applied to fiction publishing. It is easy to see how working-class subjects are excluded. Potential authors never see themselves reflected in the existing literature and therefore feel their lives provide inappropriate material to write about. The publisher finds any exploration of working-class life depressing unless it is cloaked in history or regionalism (Catherine Cookson). Colourful characters and 'warmth and humour' help, too- but who defines what is warm, colourful and humorous? And connected with this is the patronising view of what the predominantly working-class and female audience wants to read. Recently considerable Cultural Studies attention has been paid to genre fiction and in the case of feminists, romantic fiction, but I find a class sympathy often sadly lacking.

In my discussion group at the 1994 conference, I hoped to explore the first-hand experience - as writers, as readers, as cultural workers - of the working-class intellectuals gathered there. But time was short, and all the issues were pressing, so we did not have much of a chance to go into specifics. I would still like to sit some of us down and deal with questions such as: What were your earliest experiences of books? When did you first go to a library/bookshop? Do you feel comfortable in one now - what sorts? Have you ever tried to/succeeded in getting a book published with a commercial publisher? What was that experience like? What sorts of books do you like reading now? Do you, in fact, like reading? I would also look at the answers to see how they differ between women and men.

In the meantime, you might like to know that the youthful reading of this feminist intellectual included not only <u>The Panorama Book for Girls</u>, <u>Girl Annual Number Four</u>, <u>Bible Picture Stories</u>, and the <u>Princess Gift Book for Girls</u>, but also <u>Making a Car Tyre</u>, "A Dunlop Publication", and <u>Making a Foam Mattress</u> (likewise). Make of that, for the time being, what you will.

Bibliography

Olsen, Tillie. *Silences*, (1962, reprinted 1994), Virago

Luey, Beth. *Handbook for Academic Authors* (revised edition 1990- reprinted 1994) Cambridge University Press.

About the authors

The idea for this publication was formulated when we met at at a conference organised by Working Press, 'Class, Identity and Culture' in Summer 1994. We found we shared similar experiences as struggling writers from working-class backgrounds and decided to pool some of our own work to mark working-class women's achievements by publishing this book.

Sarah Richardson Merylyn Cherry
Sammy Palfrey Gail Chester
September 1995

About the FWWCP

The Federation of Worker Writers and Community Publishers is a national organisation whose main aims are:

■ To make writing and publishing accessible to all.

■ To develop and publish writing by and for working-class communities. (The Federation believes in a wide definition of working class).

■ To encourage people to take an active, co-operative and democratic role in writing, performing and publishing.

■ A commitment to equal opportunities.

Working Press is a member group of the FWWCP. For further information please contact; FWWCP, PO Box 540, Burslem, Stoke-on-Trent, ST6 6DR